*Educating Artistically Talented Students*

# Educating
## Artistically Talented Students

GILBERT CLARK
ENID ZIMMERMAN

SYRACUSE UNIVERSITY PRESS    1984

*The authors thank the following editors and publishers for permission to reprint the following material:*

Parts of Chapter 1, Part 2, were originally published in "Toward A New Conception of Talent In the Visual Arts," by Gilbert Clark and Enid Zimmerman, *Roeper Review,* 1984, *6* (4): 214–16.

Parts of Chapter 2, Part 1, were originally published in "At the Age of Six, I Gave Up a Magnificent Career As a Painter: Seventy Years of Research About Identifying Students With Superior Abilities In the Visual Arts," by Gilbert Clark and Enid Zimmerman, *Gifted Child Quarterly,* 1983, *27* (4): 180–84.

Parts of Chapter 1 and Chapter 2 will be published in "Research and Inquiry About Art Abilities and Art Talent: A Remembrance of Things Past," by Gilbert Clark and Enid Zimmerman. *Theory Into Practice,* in press, 1984.

Parts of Chapter 2, Part 4, and Figures 6, 7, and 8 were originally published in "Identifying Artistically Talented Students," by Gilbert Clark and Enid Zimmerman, *School Arts,* 1983, *83* (3): 26–31.

Table 4, "National Assessment of Educational Objectives: Outlines of Art Objectives," was adapted from National Assessment of Educational Progress, *Procedural Handbook: 1978–1979 Art Assessment.* Denver, Co: Education Commission of the States, 1981.

*The authors thank the following persons and organizations for permission to use photographs:*

Judith Burton, Boston University School Of the Arts, Boston, Massachusetts, illustration, p. 50.

Judith Coffey-Chin, Precollege Program, Rhode Island School of Design, Providence, Rhode Island, illustration, p. xiv.

David Currie, Art Department, New Trier Township High School, Winnetka, Illinois, illustration, p. 120.

Roger Jacobi, Interlochen Center For the Arts, Interlochen, Michigan, illustrations, pp. 12, 92, and 124.

**Library of Congress Cataloging in Publication Data**

Clark, Gilbert.
    Educating artistically talented students.

    Bibliography: p.
    Includes index.
      1. Gifted children—Education—United States—Art.
2. Art—Study and teaching—United States. 3. Gifted
children—Education—United States—Art—Curricula.
4. Gifted children—Identification. I. Zimmerman, Enid.
II. Title.
LC3993.265.C53 1984     371.95     84-16368
ISBN 0-8156-2320-8

*Dedicated to our Mothers*

MARY MARGARET HANNAH CLARK
ANNE KAPLAN DEUTCHMAN

*Gilbert Clark* is Professor of Art Education, Indiana University, Editor of *Art Education* (National Art Education Association), and co-author, with Dr. Zimmerman, of *Art/Design: Communicating Visually.* In 1983 he was named Indiana Art Educator of the Year. *Enid Zimmerman* is Assistant Professor of Art Education, Indiana University, and co-author of *Artstrands: A Program of Individualized Art Instruction.*

# CONTENTS

PREFACE ix

1 *Educating Artistically Talented Students* 1

PART 1 GIFTED/TALENTED EDUCATION IN THE UNITED STATES 1

PART 2 TOWARD A NEW CONCEPTION OF TALENT IN
THE VISUAL ARTS 13

PART 3 A PROGRAM STRUCTURE 27

2 *Identification* 37

PART 1 REVIEW OF IDENTIFICATION INQUIRY AND RESEARCH 37

PART 2 STUDENT CHARACTERISTICS 51

PART 3 CURRENT TESTING AND IDENTIFICATION PRACTICES 63

PART 4 RECOMMENDATIONS FOR IDENTIFICATION 73

3 *Teacher Characteristics and Teaching Strategies* 89

PART 1 REVIEW OF RESEARCH AND INQUIRY ABOUT TEACHER
CHARACTERISTICS 89

PART 2 ORIENTATIONS AND TEACHING PRACTICES 97

PART 3 RECOMMENDATIONS FOR TEACHING 105

4 *Curriculum Content* 117

PART 1 REVIEW OF RECOMMENDATIONS FOR CURRICULUM
CONTENT 117

PART 2 CONTENTS AND STRUCTURES OF CONTEMPORARY
PROGRAMS      125

PART 3 A CURRICULUM MODEL FOR LEARNING EXPERIENCES
IN THE VISUAL ARTS      133

5   *Educational Settings and
Administrative Arrangements*      143

PART 1 REVIEW OF ADMINISTRATIVE ARRANGEMENTS      143

PART 2 ADMINISTRATIVE ARRANGEMENTS AND RECOMMENDATIONS
FOR CONTEMPORARY PROGRAMS      153

6   *Looking Down the Road Ahead*      165

APPENDIX *Art Programs*      173

BIBLIOGRAPHY      177

AUTHOR INDEX      193

TOPIC INDEX      197

# PREFACE

$\mathcal{A}$RTISTICALLY TALENTED VISUAL ARTS STUDENTS in our schools are victims of many current beliefs and practices that discourage attention to their superior abilities. Such students do not receive appropriate education in their art classrooms nor do they receive the kinds of administration and program support that their exceptionality demands. Beliefs commonly held by art educators, and frequently reinforced in publications about art teaching, include several that have discouraged attention to artistically talented students. For more than thirty years, art experiences offered in schools have been viewed primarily as creative, self-expression opportunities available to all students. As a consequence, most students have been called artists and are viewed as equally creative and expressive. Art work by students, as products of self-expression activities, have become largely exempt from evaluation, criticism, or grading. As a result, the false belief that *all* students are equally talented is reinforced by lack of evaluation of their art products. A major consequence of these beliefs and practices has been a nearly total lack of education programs or special opportunities designed to meet the needs of artistically talented visual arts students.

Rampant egalitarianism should not be equated with democratic practice. In our democracy, excellence should be rewarded, not subverted; individual differences should be encouraged, not camouflaged. It is the essence of democracy that every individual has the right to achieve excellence and democratic schools should provide means for the achievement and reward of excellence. It is false to believe, however, that artistic excellence can be achieved by all, simply because the opportunity exists.

*Educating Artistically Talented Students* addresses many facets of problems related to educating children who have superior abilities in the visual arts. This book is intended, primarily, for use by elementary classroom teachers, art instructors, and junior and senior high school art teachers; it is also recommended for school administrators, gifted/talented program administrators, parents, and others who are concerned about educating artistically talented students.

*Educating Artistically Talented Students* is organized into six chapters:

## Chapter 1. *Educating Artistically Talented Students*

In Part 1, Gifted/Talented Education in the United States, a general background is presented summarizing the history of education for students who are gifted. This chapter is intended to provide a context for understanding problems about artistically talented students. Part 2, Toward a New Conception of Talent in the Visual Arts, helps dispel popular misunderstandings about children with superior abilities in the visual arts. Part 3 presents a program structure for artistically talented students in which major orientations and components of a model for a program are discussed.

## Chapter 2. *Identification*

In Part 1, Review of Identification Inquiry and Research, 100 years of inquiry about identifying students with superior abilities in the visual arts is reviewed. Part 2, Student Characteristics, presents an extended list of characteristics derived from the historical survey in Part 1. Part 3, Current Testing and Identification Practices, reports practical identification devices and methods that are currently being used. In Part 4, Recommendations for Identification, identification procedures and methods are summarized and recommendations for effective and efficient identification practices are made.

## Chapter 3. *Teacher Characteristics and Teaching Strategies*

Review of Research and Inquiry about Teacher Characteristics, Part 1, summarizes research and inquiry from the past and lists ideal characteristics of teachers of artistically talented students. In Part 2, Orientations and Teaching Practices, current teaching strategies used in programs for teaching artistically talented students are reported. Part 3, Recommendations for Teaching, uses information from the first two parts to summarize and make recommendations about teachers for artistically talented students.

Chapter 4. *Curriculum Content*

Review of Recommendations for Curriculum Content, Part 1, presents past inquiry about the content of art programs for artistically talented students. In Part 2, Content and Structure of Contemporary Programs, current art content used in art programs for artistically talented students is discussed. Part 3, A Curriculum Model for Learning Experiences in the Visual Arts, presents a model for organizing sequential art content in educational programs for artistically talented students. Parts 1, 2, and 3 are summarized and recommendations are made about curriculum content for artistically talented students in Part 4, Summary and Recommendations.

Chapter 5. *Educational Settings and Administrative Arrangements*

A list of educational settings and arrangements for talented students is formulated from a review of research and inquiry presented in Part 1, Review of Administrative Arrangements. Part 2, Administrative Arrangements and Recommendations for Contemporary Programs, presents educational settings and arrangements in current practice and summarizes and makes recommendations for future practices.

Chapter 6. *Looking Down the Road Ahead*

A generalized summary of major issues and findings in this text is presented along with suggestions and recommendations for present and future decisions about educating artistically talented students.

An Appendix lists the art programs that have been referred to in this book.

*Educating Artistically Talented Students*

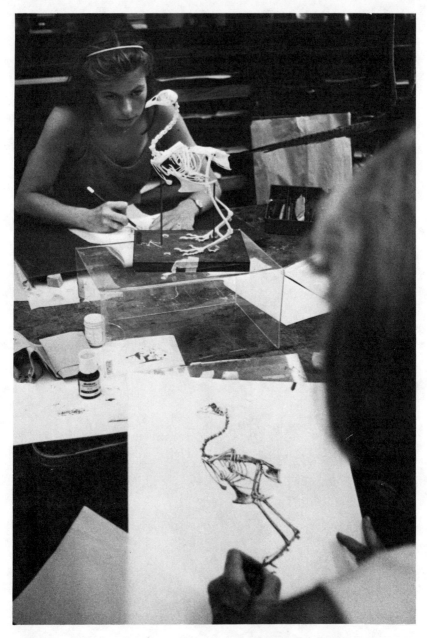

These students are drawing in the Nature Lab of the Rhode Island School of Design as part of their pre-college program. The Nature Lab is a resource center and studio where a great number of varied nature specimens are housed. Such drawing requires careful perception and understanding along with mastery of drawing techniques and media. Photo by David Witbeck.

# Educating Artistically Talented Students

PART I GIFTED/TALENTED EDUCATION
IN THE UNITED STATES

*P*ROBLEMS OF IDENTIFYING and providing appropriate educational programs to students with superior abilities in the visual arts are clearly related to similar and unresolved problems in education of academically gifted students. In order to create a context for understanding the present, in which talent in art is often viewed as an outgrowth of free expression and determined solely by heredity, it is necessary to know how giftedness has been viewed and identified in the past. It has been pointed out, perhaps too many times, that education is cyclic; that popular educational themes and practices recur in fifteen-, twenty-, or thirty-year cycles.

Historical study of the concept of genius, as it was discussed and studied in the middle and late 19th century, and study of the effects of measurement and testing, in the early 20th century, reveals two major influences that have effected the present character of the education of gifted/ talented students in our schools. The frequent separation of academic and artistic pursuits as wholly different from one another is only a recent phenomenon and one which has had many detrimental effects on education in the arts.

## THE CONCEPT OF GENIUS

Between 1850 and 1900, many Europeans, and a few Americans, studied people of genius and wrote tracts on the concept of genius. At the same time, the concept of "stupidity" or "feeble mindedness" was also being examined. Tests for measuring degrees of intelligence, academic abilities, or talent in the arts, however, did not yet exist. As a result, untenable claims about genius and stupidity were made freely and frequently. At this time, genius was a term applied commonly to superior writers, painters, mathematicians, sculptors, composers, philosophers, and all persons of exceptional talent and achievement. There were no differentiations made between academic and artistic achievement.

In 1869, Francis Galton wrote *Hereditary Genius* in which he reported his study of characteristics of men of genius. In this work, Galton established foundations for the measurement of intelligence, though he did not carry this work to realization. Galton studied families, especially the offspring of famous persons, and thereby opened the door for scientific study of children and of their intelligence. His correlations of intelligence to sensory discrimination abilities and psycho-motor skills and his proposition that certain measurable abilities could be used to predict intelligence were major guideposts in development of the testing of intelligence.

In contrast to the systematic and empirical studies of Galton, another work of this time was Cesare Lombrosco's *The Man of Genius* (1895). In this fascinating book, Lombrosco reports his historical study of many men of genius of the past. In accord with commonly held ideas, Lombrosco claimed that genius and insanity are closely related. Genius is equated with neuroses, morbidity, criminality, sterility, somnambulism, physical abnormality, madness of all kinds, immorality, emaciation, deficient speech, schizophrenia, amnesia, and stupidity in everyday affairs. This is not the complete list of characteristics Lombrosco managed to report, but it does typify the popular conception of genius as reported by Lombrosco and others. Even to think with intensity is equated with insanity: "It is very true that nothing so much resembles a person attacked by madness as a man of genius when meditating or moulding his conceptions" (Lombrosco 1895, p. 22).

## THE MEASUREMENT OF INTELLIGENCE

In a complex history, often credited to have its origins in the work of Galton, the measurement of intelligence evolved over a number of years and grew from the work of many people. Each contribution added to the international understanding of intelligence, recognition of the fact that intelligence is normally distributed, and that retardation and giftedness are extremes of this distribution.

Building on a developmental history of related efforts of others, Alfred Binet and Theophile Simon were commissioned, in 1904, to develop procedures for identifying mentally deficient students in order to segregate them in the schools of Paris. Binet was a psychologist who had studied abnormal psychology and through test development studies (i.e., Binet and Henri 1896) had become very interested in individual differences. Simon, a physician, was selected to work with Binet because mental deficiency was considered a physical abnormality in the early part of the twentieth century. In 1905, Binet and Simon published their first graded scale of tasks and age norms so that each subject's performance could be evaluated. In subsequent test versions, published in 1908, and 1911, their identification task shifted to include describing individual differences among normal children, as well as the mentally deficient, and to validate their assignments of task to age levels. Out of these efforts, the mental age concept, in which task achievements are compared to age norms, was contributed and verified.

A number of Americans, some of whom were studying in Europe, adapted Binet's tests. The major figure in this group was Lewis Terman. At about the same time that Binet was revising the first Binet and Simon tests, Terman was studying "brighter" and "stupid" boys in a local school near Clark University, Massachusetts (Terman 1906). In this research, Terman was studying a number of test tasks grouped into factors, though Binet had studied a number of separate tasks. Terman correlated the results on all of his factors and concluded that a single measurement of "intelligence" was possible. He transformed the Binet Tests, by dropping, editing, or adapting Binet's items, and adding items of his own design, into the first Stanford-Binet Scale in 1916. Working at Stanford University, Terman and Maud Merrill subsequently issued two more revisions of their intelligence test (Terman and Merrill 1937, 1960).

The other major figure in early development of the testing of intelligence was David Wechsler. He, and others, questioned the unity of all of Terman's test items as factors of intelligence. Wechsler designed a test in which the same verbal and performance items were administered to all testees of all ages. His desire was to measure the same abilities at all ages and this led to creation of an adult version of the test (WAIS) and another version for children (WISC) (Wechsler 1958). Both the Wechsler and Terman and Merrill tests continue to be used today in individual testing of intelligence. There have been, of course, a number of tests developed to measure intelligence since Terman's and Wechsler's basic work. Guilford's (1967) continuing development of tasks to measure achievement of each of the 120 factors of the Structure of the Intellect model, Wechsler's Preschool and Primary Scale of Intelligence (WPPSI) (Wechsler 1967), and

Kaufman's Assessment Battery for Children (K-ABC) (Kaufman and Kaufman 1983) are indications of the continuing search for accurate measurement of intelligence across all age groups. Hawthorne, Speer, and Buccellanto (1983) question whether the WPPSI subtests have items of adequate difficulty for assessing the abilities of gifted children. The K-ABC, designed for 2½ to 12½ year olds, demonstrates an interest in minimizing the role of language and verbal skills for successful performance. On this assessment instrument, intelligence is viewed as a style of solving problems and processing information.

In 1926, Florence Goodenough published the first *Draw-a-Man-Test*. This test demonstrated that drawings by children displayed their cognitive abilities more than their aesthetic sensibilities. Goodenough, a student of Terman, was originally interested in measuring intelligence with drawings and studying children's drawings as they reflected each child's personality and interests. In addition to using the *Draw-a-Man-Test* to determine personality traits, Goodenough concluded that keen powers of observation and a good memory for details are factors that produce high scores on the test, rather than artistic ability. Dale Harris (1963) worked with Goodenough in revising the *Draw-a-Man-Test*. He felt that children's drawings could be used to determine their intellectual maturity and that children's drawings of the human figure could be used as an index of their general concept formation abilities. Both Goodenough and Harris emphasized that the *Draw-a-Man-Test* does not measure talent or aptitude for drawing.

There are two reasons for telling this history in a book about teaching artistically talented students. One is that it may be unfamiliar history to some readers. The other is to point out that artistic tasks somehow were left out of the search for intelligence. Though Binet and Henri (1896) had included some artistic and aesthetic tasks in their early work, such tasks fell by the wayside in subsequent history of intelligence testing. As a result, giftedness has become equated with superior verbal and numeric skills and artistic talent has become disassociated from intellectual achievement. Despite current attempts to critique and correct this situation, by Guilford (1967) and others, the popular conception of genius or giftedness has come to be defined as high scores on an individually administered intelligence test.


## THE GENETIC STUDIES OF GENIUS

Another factor that contributed significantly to the current definition of giftedness is Terman's monumental study of over 1500 subjects defined by their high scores on the Stanford-Binet Scale. The *Genetic Studies of Genius* began in 1921 with a $20,000 grant from the Commonwealth Fund. It is an ongoing, longitudinal study that began with 1,528 children who scored 140 or more points on the Stanford-Binet intelligence scale. The purpose of this research is to identify and study this group without doing any special educational intervention. People in the original group, and their children and grandchildren, continue to be studied. The six volumes of the *Genetic Studies of Genius* report the first data collection (Terman 1925), study of a select subgroup within the study (Cox 1926), a five-year follow-up (Terman, Burks, and Jensen 1930), a twenty-five year follow-up (Terman and Oden 1947), a thirty-five year follow-up (Terman and Oden 1959), and a forty-year follow-up (Oden 1968). A new volume is currently pending. No other group of gifted individuals has been studied so intensively or over such a long period of time. The study is planned to continue until the last members of the original group are deceased.

The *Genetic Studies of Genius* has done much to describe and characterize giftedness and contribute to our understanding of gifted persons. For instance, Cox (1926) disputed most of the claims of Lombrosco and others and showed that highly gifted children possess many favorable characteristics such as superior physical maturation, social development, general health, positive personality, initiative, perseverance, and intellectual zeal. These findings were established from longitudinal study of over 100 individuals identified as superior with the Stanford-Binet Scale. These and other findings from the *Genetic Studies of Genius* continue to contribute to our understanding of the need for special educational provisions for gifted students because of their unique abilities, and our knowledge that such students will have an impact on our society as adult leaders. Terman reported: "If we dispense with sociological formulations, the question immediately arises of the 'mute inglorious' genius whose potentialities never flowered. . . . The concept of unfulfilled genius has theoretical validity, and society's failure to bring out the potentialities of many of its best minds has rueful significance" (Terman and Burks 1933).

Today's task is to apply this same injunction in the name of the "mute inglorious" artist-genius whose potentialities never flowered. The artistically gifted/talented child as potential artist and important contributor to American society and culture needs to be reawakened and restored. False distinctions between intellectual and artistic achievement need to be re-examined and tested. Jerome Bruner (1962) describes the problem this way: "The scientist and the poet do not live at antipodes . . . the artificial separation of the two modes of knowing cripples the contemporary intellectual as an effective myth maker for his times" (pp. 2–3).

## TESTING OF ART ABILITIES

Another important movement needs to be reported in this brief synopsis, the short lived history of testing of various aspects of art abilities apart from the testing of intelligence. In 1919, a major work entitled *Classes for Gifted Children* (Whipple 1919) reported eighty-eight different tests used in diagnosis, identification, and placement of gifted children in public schools in Urbana, Illinois. Many tests are described in this book that have since disappeared. These include the Manuel Perceptual Learning Test, the Steacy Drawing Construction Tests, the Drawing a Church, Snowball Fight, Horse, and Toy Wagon tests, Thorndike's Esthetic Appreciation Test, and other tests of artistic abilities. During the early 1900s, the testing of art abilities was considered both possible and practical. Whipple had a chapter in his book entitled "An Analytic Study of Talent in Drawing" that is introduced with this statement: "It was felt that the study of the selection and training of gifted children ought to be supplemented by a study of the restricted sort of superiority that we designate as 'talent'. For several reasons talent in drawing, as revealed under school conditions, seemed a promising field for such a study" (Whipple 1919, p. 126).

Forty-five separate tests related to art abilities were reported in this chapter! With the exception of the Stanford-Binet, none of these tests are used today. Yet, all of the following inferences were drawn from this important study:

1. The term "drawing" applies to a very complex process, and the production of an effective drawing calls into operation a number of varied and distinguishable operations.
2. Correspondingly, persons "talented" in drawing exhibit marked individual differences in their mental and physical characteristics.
3. Any statement of the essential characteristics of persons talented in drawing presuppose a statement of the particular type of drawing ability that is exhibited.
4. A certain elementary ability in graphic representation . . . may exist more or less independently of general mental ability.
5. But ability (a) to acquire the advanced technique into which conceptual factors enter or (b) to create original drawings of merit implies the existence of a good degree of general intelligence.
6. Linguistic ability . . . is not correlated with ability in

drawing, [it] may or may not be associated with ability to draw.

7. The sort of motor ability present in drawing is not revealed by any of the stock tests of "motor ability."

8. Persons who exhibit talent in drawing show no uniform tendency to write well; handwriting and drawing are relatively independent performances.

9. There is some evidence . . . that flexibility of motor habit . . . may be exhibited more decidedly in persons talented in drawing than in persons not talented in drawing.

10. The ability to discriminate fine differences in distances, lengths, curves and proportions . . . is not satisfactorily measured for diagnostic purposes.

11. Despite individual differences, tests of "observation" . . . appear to have some value for the diagnosis of ability in drawing.

12. Introspective reports . . . indicate that while many who are talented in drawing have superior visual imagery . . . the same thing may be said for kinesthetic imagery.

13/14. Memory for visual forms (and ability to manipulate spatial forms mentally) is worth testing for drawing ability. . . .

15/16. [discusses tests of questionable value and concludes that] . . . skill in drawing may co-exist with poor esthetic taste.
(Whipple 1919, pp. 135–39)

These 1919 inferences are interesting because they offer a picture of some of the possibilities that rigorous research might establish or reaffirm in the 1980s. The second, third, and fourth decades of the 1900s were witness to innumerable research and test development efforts towards describing talent in the visual arts. Ayer (1916), Manuel (1919a, 1919b), and Whipple (1919) at the University of Illinois, and Meier (1926, 1939, 1942, Tiebout and Meier 1936) and Seashore (1942), at the University of Iowa, were active in leading numerous studies toward defining and identifying talent in the arts. At the same period of time, numerous other persons were developing various tests of artistic abilities. Helga Eng reported her studies of *The Psychology of Children's Drawings* in 1931. She stated:

It may be objected, it is true, that the mental process behind the child's drawing is a special and peculiar one, so that no conclusion can be arrived at concerning general mental development from an examination of a drawing. The fact that this objection does not hold good is shown by the wide parallelism that can be proved to exist between the child's drawing and its speech, its formation of concepts and its thinking. (Eng 1931, p. 181)

Numerous persons agreed with this assertion during the 1920s, 1930s, and early 1940s. This was a period of active test development in the visual arts. Standardized tests and idiosyncratic tests designed by researchers became available for research about visual arts abilities. Major tests developed during these decades were:

> *The Lewerenz Tests in Fundamental Abilities in the Visual Arts*
>     (Lewerenz 1927)
> *Meier Art Tests* (Meier 1929)
> *McAdory Art Test* (McAdory 1929)
> *Knauber Art Ability* and *Art Vocabulary Tests* (Knauber 1932)
> *Measuring Scale for Freehand Drawing. Part II, Design and*
>     *Composition* (Kline & Carey 1933)
> *The Horn Art Aptitude Scale* (Horn 1935)
> *Selective Art Aptitude Test* (Varnum 1939)
> *Graves Design Judgment Test* (Graves 1948)

Of these, several are out of print and several are still in use. Khatena (1982) discusses use of the Knauber, Meier, and Horn tests for identification of visual arts talent, though he does qualify their application at this time. Buros (1972, 1974) and Eisner (1972) have evaluated most of these tests for general or specific use and their present applicability. Instrument development that is consistent with the most current concerns of researchers in the field of art talent and art development is generally lacking. Khatena contends that "identification of able students in art is . . . difficult. There is no completely satisfactory test of aptitude in art, especially during the school years of individuals" (Khatena 1982, p. 94).

Terman's Stanford-Binet Scale made possible the identification of students with high IQs that was the foundation of the *Genetic Studies of Genius*. No such instruments exist, at this time, with equal power for identification of students with superior gifts or talents in the visual arts. Small wonder that superior art abilities have become disassociated from intellectual giftedness or genius. Superior art ability, and especially precocious achievement in visual arts, is often poorly recognized and commonly misunderstood, as was intelligence and precocious intellectual achievement in the first part of this century.

Various aspects of the Torrance Test of Creative Thinking (Torrance 1966, 1974) and Guilford's Creativity Tests for Children (1973) have been recommended for diagnosing art abilities. It is questionable, however, that art ability can be predicted from these creativity tests.

## CREATIVITY AND SELF-EXPRESSION
## IN THE VISUAL ARTS

Beginning with the Child Study Movement of the turn-of-the-century, led by G. Stanley Hall, and peaking as art education constructs in the writings of Cole (1940, 1966), Viola (1942), D'Amico (1942), Lowenfeld (1954), and Lowenfeld and Brittain (1947, 1952, 1957, 1964, 1975), *all* children came to be viewed as creative, self-expressive artists by art teachers and educators alike. This conception dominated the field of art education during the late 1940s, 1950s, 1960s, and 1970s. Directive teaching was seen as imposition of adult standards. Ability testing was seen as inequitable and thwarting to the child. Evaluation of children's art work was seen as adult imposition, frustrating to the child, and inequitable and unfair. Directive teaching, ability testing, and evaluation of children's work, though commonly practiced in other school subjects, were considered detrimental to creativity and the unfettered self-expression in art that was so highly valued at this time. The power and ubiquity of creativity and self-expression in the practice of art education was evidenced everywhere (Eisner 1972). Books, curriculum guides, magazine and journal articles, and oral presentations at art teachers' conventions echoed these sentiments over and over again. The pervasiveness of concern for student creativity and self-expression explains the abrupt stopping of test development in the visual arts and subsequent confounding of giftedness, creativity, and talent in the arts.

During the 1940s, Torrance and many others developed what became known as creativity tests and creativity became an educational byword. These creativity tests were used to measure problem solving skills and divergent thinking abilities applicable to all kinds of situations. They did not, however, measure art judgment or art making skills. Though the concept of creativity is poorly understood and poorly defined (Wallach and Kogan 1965), it became a major rationale for art education programs taught in the schools (Eisner 1972). Unfortunately, the confounding of giftedness, creativity, and talent in the arts remains. It is clear, however, from analysis by Wallach and Kogan (1965), Guilford (1967), and others that creativity as measured on tests of creativity and various abilities in the arts are separable and only nominally related.


## ACHIEVEMENT TESTS

Development of successful intelligence tests for individuals led, inevitably, to group tests and standarized tests of achievement. As intelligence tests verified degrees of individual differences, researchers began to look for similar instruments that would explain individual differences between achievement in various school subjects. *The Stanford Achievement Tests, Metropolitan Achievement Tests, California Achievement Tests,* and the *SRA Achievement Series* are well known to most educators. These tests measure student achievement of knowledge and skills in common school subjects as reading, science, arithmetic and mathematics, language arts, social studies, and handwriting. The visual arts, however, have not been incorporated into any of the standardized achievement tests used by schools.

Achievement tests have profoundly effected organization and content of school curricula. School programs in major school subjects are designed that enable students to achieve knowledges and skills such tests measure. Funding is provided to purchase textbooks, study materials, audiovisual materials, and other supportive devices for reading, spelling, arithmetic and mathematics, science, and other subjects that will be tested by standardized achievement tests. In self protection, schools are compelled to insure as much student success on these measures as possible.


## SUMMARY AND CONCLUSIONS

Measurements of intelligence and achievement have been developed over the past 120 years. Parallel or similar development of identification procedures and education programs for students with superior talent in the visual arts has not occurred. Efforts toward program funding, public support, development of teaching strategies, program content, and educational settings for students who are talented in the visual arts has lagged behind most other subject matters offered in the schools. They lack a similar foundation of valid tests, longitudinal studies, and other in-depth research. Programs that emphasize differential achievement and reward superior performance in the visual arts are not common. Art teachers do not usually have access to strategies and resources that are appropriate to educate their most talented students. The school environment is not often one that nurtures or facilitates education of highly able visual arts students. Parents of students with superior abilities in the arts are often forced to seek instructional resources outside the school setting (Bloom 1982). In many communities, these resources do not exist; if they do, they are offered on a very limited basis.

It is hoped that in the 1980s, there will be renewed interest, research, development, and support of programs for students with superior talent in the visual arts. Long neglected, this group offers an exciting potential for study and program development. It is hoped that a new page in the history of education of student talented in the arts is about to be written.

This student at the Interlochen Center for the Arts is surrounded by her paintings and drawings in her studio–work space. The sophistication of her art works and her intense concentration are indicators of her abilities as an artistically talented student. Photo by Brill.

PART 2 TOWARD A NEW CONCEPTION OF TALENT
IN THE VISUAL ARTS

*T*HERE ARE MANY POPULAR MISCONCEPTIONS that are commonly believed about characteristics and abilities of artistically talented students. Some of these misconceptions relate to identifying talented students,
providing educational services for these students, and the teaching of artistically talented students.

Many people believe that art work of artistically talented students
is easy to recognize in a classroom. Many students, however, demonstrate
their art talents in activities that do not occur at school and teachers are
often unaware of the rich visual expressions that students create outside
the classroom (Wilson and Wilson 1976). Many students, especially adolescents, have learned to mask their art abilities because such abilities may
be seen as strange or be otherwise misunderstood by teachers and other
students. Students who perform well in the art classroom and who conform closely to classroom expectations are often judged to be talented. Thus,
conformity may be confused with talent and non-conformity may be con-
founded, by the teacher, as indicating lack of talent but these are poor criteria for identification of highly talented students. The obvious difficulties
of such confusion have been noted by many researchers. Gallagher (1975)
has pointed out many gifted/talented children remain unrecognized in school
because their school performance is inconsistent to teachers' expectations.
Fine (1970) noted that many children demonstrate superior achievement
only outside the school (i.e., in extracurricular activities) because such
achievements are more rewarding, gratifying, and less threatening, than
those called for in the school classroom.

A second common misunderstanding is that above average intelligence is not a requirement for superior artistic performance. The argument has been stated many ways. As recently as the 1960s, prominent educators have claimed that intelligence tests "do not give any indication of
artistic giftedness" (Lowenfeld and Brittain 1964, p. 382), or that there are
some children with high musical or artistic or mechanical ability and average or below average intellectual ability (DeHaan and Havighurst 1961).
One consequence of this misunderstanding is reinforced when schools place
students with low intellectual abilities in art classes with the belief that such
children can succeed in art though they may not succeed in other academic

subjects. An even more detrimental practice is the opposite of this in which all students with superior intellectual abilities are counselled away from art classes in the belief that art classes can make no contribution to the needs of such students.

Arbitrary separation of intelligence and artistic performance has been questioned and challenged for many years (Arnheim 1969). In 1936, Tiebout and Meier summarized results of their own years of research and concluded that artistic potential and achievement in art are largely dependent upon intellectual capacity. A number of art educators have noted that a positive relationship exists between intelligence and ability in art (Klar and Winslow 1933; Tiebout and Meier 1936; Ziegfeld 1961; Gaitskell and Hurwitz 1970). Other researchers have shown that most high IQ students are also talented and that most talented students also have high IQs (Fritz 1930; Schubert 1973; Vernon, Adamson, & Vernon 1977). Though superior intelligence and superior art abilities are clearly interdependent, not all children with a high IQ possess art talent. All children with superior art talent, however, do possess a higher than average IQ (Manuel 1919a; Hollingworth 1926; Schubert 1973; Luca and Allen 1974). A higher than average IQ has been described as a necessary condition, by several of the researchers cited, for acquiring the advanced techniques and skills that are required for superior art work.

The adult artist is often caricatured in Western cultures as a social outcast or misfit, a flagrant nonconformist, or as a loner who is out of touch with reality. Children with superior artistic abilities often suffer from misapplications of these caricatures by adults. Just as these caricatures of the artist are most often false, so is the stereotype of gifted or talented children as socially inept, physically immature, or emotionally unstable. Numerous studies of gifted and talented children have refuted these common stereotypes. Research has shown that, generally, gifted and talented students are social and intellectual leaders, physically superior to their peers, and emotionally well-adjusted (Terman 1925; Terman and Oden 1947; Witty 1951; Clark 1979; Tuttle and Becker 1980). A too-common stereotype of the talented child as a social isolate occurs frequently. This misconception is refuted by evidence that gifted and talented students are chosen, frequently, as preferred companions in school and by the above average frequency of their social contacts and relationships (Grace and Booth 1958; Miller 1956; Gallagher 1979).

A major misunderstanding, often reinforced in art education literature, is that talented students need no instruction or that instruction in the arts is harmful. Statements such as "One cannot teach art. Nobody can. . . . Artists are born" (Viola 1942, p. 35), "Let children do what they please, their creativity should be entirely unconstrained" (Fritz 1930, p. 22), and "where rigid plans are made . . . then the experience may be disappointing and frustrating to the children" (Brittain 1961, p. 283) have led teachers to believe that children with art talents should not be taught art or that art talent will develop and improve simply as a consequence of maturation. As a result of belief in this misunderstanding, teachers have been told that talented children can make it on their own or that they do not need special help in the schools (Meredith and Landin 1957; Jackson 1979). A further application of this misunderstanding is that educational programs for artistically talented students need not be planned and that a supply of available art materials is all that is required to meet the needs of talented students (Laycock 1957; Brittain 1961; Tempest 1974).

It is surprising that the previously discussed misunderstandings are still commonly held and are frequently restated in current literature, because studies of talented students show, over and over again, that directive education is essential to the development of superior abilities (Feldman 1979; Robinson, Roedell, and Jackson 1979). Talent in the arts must be encouraged, exercised, and practiced in order to flourish (Ashley 1973) and students with superior abilities need differentiated assignments, time schedules, and instructional guidance (Boas, 1927; Luca and Allen 1974; Eisner 1966; Salome 1974). The Marland Report, which established superior abilities in the visual and performing arts as a subset of giftedness, asserted that talented children require differentiated educational programs and services beyond those normally provided by the school program (Marland 1972).

Many people still believe that every child in school is equally talented or that only a very few children are endowed with art talent. Believing either of these misconceptions predicates against sound education in the arts and leads to educational programs that are detrimental to the needs of superior students. Believing that all children are equally talented leads to non-instructional programs in which simply providing materials is sufficient for artistic performance or that children's art work should never be evaluated. Believing that only a few children can ever be artistically capable leads to total rejection of art as school content or to programs that favor only a few students and fail to meet the needs of other students. These misconceptions are stated by teachers as "all children are creative," "art is merely a way to express feelings and moods," "Everyone can draw," and children often state that "I can't draw a straight line," "don't look at my work," and, ultimately, "I just can't make anything look right."

## CLARIFYING THE CONCEPT OF ARTISTIC TALENT

Intelligence is a fairly universal concept. It has been defined for a long time as a score, plus or minus ten, on a standardized intelligence test. It is not disputed, in most academic circles, that the intelligence quotient, or IQ, is relatively stable, accurately predictive of many other behaviors that are related to intelligence, and that a person's IQ reflects his or her genetic and environmental backgrounds in, roughly, a 70%–30% proportion (Wechsler 1958; Guilford 1967). Intelligence is normally distributed; it is commonly agreed that an individual who has been carefully tested with an intelligence test will have a score somewhere on a broad scale of normally distributed scores. Some people will receive a low score, most people will receive an average score, and some people will receive a high score. Intelligence, therefore, is a construct that includes many deviations above or below a mean, and IQ is often stated in terms of deviation from the mean. Giftedness, as a human characteristic, is frequently defined as two or three standard deviations above the mean (see Figure 1).

Research not yet carried out might also establish that art talent, like intelligence, is normally distributed in the world's population (Burt 1967). If accurate, valid, and reliable instruments for the measurement of art talent were available, as they are for the measurement of intelligence,

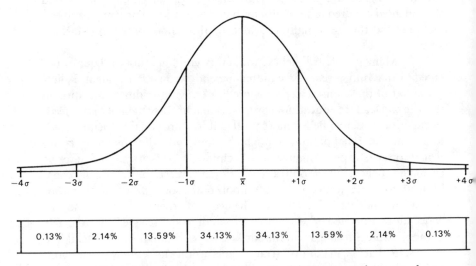

FIGURE 1. Normal distribution, mean and standard deviations, and percent of cases under portions of the normal curve.

it could be determined whether some people have very little, most people have an average amount, and whether some people have a very great deal of art talent. It is purely a conjecture, at this time, whether art talent is normally distributed, but it is an idea that is clearly worth examining further.

Peterson's *Early Conceptions and Tests of Intelligence,* printed in 1925, discussed the concept of intelligence and the development of intelligence tests up to the early 1920s (Peterson 1925). Our understanding of art talent as a construct or as a measurable human trait is, in 1983, very comparable to the understanding of intelligence that Peterson reported in 1925. There is access, now, to conjecture and analytic writings and to isolated, idiosyncratic research reports that have sought answers to diverse problems relative to understanding and measuring art behaviors. Present knowledge about art talent is similar to the knowledge of intelligence reported by Peterson; it is fragmentary and incomplete. The sophisticated knowledge and understanding of intelligence, reported thirty or forty years after Peterson's book by Wechsler (1958), Guilford (1967), Brown (1965), Piaget (1966), and others is evidence of what are mere possibilities, at this time, in pursuit of knowledge and understanding of art talent.

## ASPECTS OF ART TALENT

The artistically gifted/talented child has been discussed in the literature of art education by various researchers, psychologists, teachers, and theorists. The results are fascinating though they are often contradictory: one of the more fundamental findings of researchers relates to the concept of art talent as a normally distributed trait. The finding is that all differences in drawing skills and art behaviors of highly able and less able students are differences in degree and not in kind. For example, all children develop their own style of drawing though some will develop a qualitatively richer style than others. Ernst Meumann (1912), a German psychologist and educator, studied observable differences between behaviors of highly able and less able groups of art students and subsequently described eleven causes of inefficiency in drawing. Meumann reported that all behaviors in drawing are observable across all students and, therefore, no behaviors in drawing are exclusive to the highly able or the less able. That is a fascinating report that has been reiterated by a number of other researchers. Meier and Seashore, in early studies relative to artistic talents, reported several times that differences between students with varying degrees of talent were differences in degree and not in kind (Meier 1930, 1939). Under the leadership of Munro, Lark-Horovitz and other persons studied artistically talented and average students in classes at the Cleveland Museum of Art and in Cleveland's public schools. Summative reports of these research studies by Munro, Lark-Horovitz, and others frequently reported that all differences between "indifferent," "average," "special," and "remarkable" students (those were categoric descriptors used by the researchers) were differences in degree and not in kind (Lark-Horovitz 1937, 1941; Lark-Horovitz, Barnhart, and Sills 1939; Lark-Horovitz and Norton 1959, 1960; Lark-Horovitz, Lewis, and Luca 1967; Munro 1956).

Another contribution to understanding of talent as a normally distributed construct can be deduced from studies by the National Assessment of Educational Progress (NAEP): *Design and Drawing Skills* (1977) and *Art and Young Americans* (1981a). These reports are based, in part, upon the administration of design and drawing exercises that measured students' art production abilities. These production exercises do not measure the range of possible art production assignments, yet they do tax the skills and abilities of students and yield a scale of naive to sophisticated solutions relative to each problem.

NAEP art assessments demonstrated that scales could be constructed indicating naive to sophisticated solutions to problems and that students' solutions could be placed in graded categories along each scale. Students' solutions to problems posed as production tasks were different in degree, therefore implying a range of solutions that could be divided into categories of different levels of achievement.

Neither children nor adults are intelligent or not-intelligent, nor are they talented or not-talented. Things are not that simple. Intelligence is measured on a scale that ranges from minimum intelligence, to average intelligence, to maximum intelligence. It is, therefore, not true that all children are gifted. It is true that all children are intelligent, they possess some degree of intelligence that effectively controls and limits their capabilities to learn and to function as human beings. All children may possess art talent in much the same way. If art talent is normally distributed on a scale that ranges from minimum, to average, to maximum talent, the amount of art talent each person possesses will effectively control and limit his or her capabilities to learn and to perform tasks related to art.

## DIMENSIONS OF ARTISTIC BEHAVIORS

We created an art education content model in which we advocated the design of curricula that acknowledges entering level, beginning art students as naive in their understandings about art (Clark and Zimmerman 1978a). From this naive stage, learning experiences and teacher interventions move learners through a series of stages that culminate in attainment of sophistication of learning about art. In this model, the learner moves from a hypothetical naive stage (NN) to a still predominantly naive stage (NNs) in which the learner requires introductory, readiness-building learning experiences. These experiences decrease the learner's naiveté and contribute to his or her budding sophistication. At a subsequent stage (Ns), the learner's decreased naiveté and emerging sophistication prepare him or her for intermediate level learnings. At the intermediate state (NsSn), the learner's skill development and maturity of learning show some evidence of sophistication but also evidence further need for learning. More demanding teacher interventions and learning experiences decrease naiveté until the learner reaches a state (Sn) in which sophisticated skills and learnings predominate. Further learning leads to the attainment of understandings and skills at a stage (SnS) where sophistication is demonstrated at a near mastery level. We have outlined generalized curriculum content for teaching of art for each of these stages based upon learning about the adult, professional roles of artist, art historian, art critic, and aesthetician (Clark and Zimmerman 1978a, 1981).

This model (Figure 2) can be used to create an organizing framework for reporting completed research relative to art talent, identify needed research, and define art talent as a normally distributed concept. If the five stages of naive to sophisticated attainment are superimposed over a normal distribution (Figure 3), the standard deviations might be seen as describing parallel levels of the development of talent.

Fitting some work by other researchers into this organizing schema may make it possible to define art talent as a normally distributed concept. For instance, categoric descriptors and descriptions of learner behaviors used by reporters of the Cleveland studies might be seen as describing four of the five naive to sophisticated stages outlined above (Figure 4).

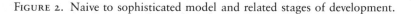

| NN | NsN | Ns | NsSn | Sn | SnS | SS |
|---|---|---|---|---|---|---|
| Naive | Introductory | Rudimentary | Intermediate | Advanced | Mastery-level | Sophisticated |

FIGURE 2. Naive to sophisticated model and related stages of development.

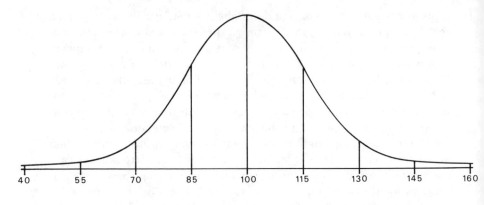

FIGURE 3. Normal distribution, deviation IQs, naive to sophisticated model, and related stages of development.

This is important because it implies that researchers could compile results of art production and perception tasks and categorically group resulting products or measures as evidence of naive to sophisticated abilities in art. As this possibility emerges, we can begin to think of art talent as a normally distributed concept with predictable deviations above and below a mean. Superimposition of naive to sophisticated stages and group-

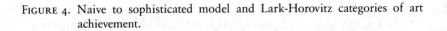

FIGURE 4. Naive to sophisticated model and Lark-Horovitz categories of art achievement.

ings of naive to sophisticated products or behaviors on a normal distribution produces a new model for the identification of artistically superior students as those who demonstrate special to remarkable qualities on art tasks.

This conception accommodates new interpretations of the results of previous research and provides a schema whereby those results have new meanings relative to the teaching and learning of artistically superior students. For instance, Meumann's (1912) research listed eleven causes of inefficiency in drawing. They can be seen as describing predominantly naive (NNs) drawing skills. In contrast, it is possible to restate the factors as behavioral descriptors of sophisticated (SnS) drawing skills. The following lists show Meumann's causes of inefficiency in drawing on the left and, on the right, we have rewritten each factor as a sophisticated drawing skill:

| Meumann: Factors of Naive Drawing Skill (NNs) | Clark and Zimmerman: Factors of Sophisticated Drawing Skill (SnS) |
|---|---|
| The will to analyze and to notice forms and colors has not been stimulated. | The will to notice and analyze forms and colors is aroused. |
| The intention to analyze may be aroused, and yet the individual may find the analysis too difficult. | The intention to analyze is aroused and is practiced with success. |
| The memory of that to be represented may be deficient. It may be incomplete or vague in form or in color. The memory of spatial relations may be inadequate. | The memory of that to be represented is complete and correct in respect to form, color, and spatial relationships. |
| There may be lack of ability to hold the image during the act of drawing. | The ability to visualize an image during the act of drawing exists and is practiced until completion of the drawing. |
| The memory image and the perceptual image may not be coordinated with the movements in drawing. | The memory image and the perceptual image are congruent and successfully delineated by the movements in drawing. |
| The sight of the drawing in its imperfection as compared with the memory image may disturb the image. | The sight of the drawing is accepted as congruent, compared with the memory image, and does not disturb the student. |

| Meumann: Factors of Naive Drawing Skill (NNs) | Clark and Zimmerman: Factors of Sophisticated Drawing Skill (SnS) |
|---|---|
| The drawer may lack schemata on which to found his drawing. | The student generates a variety of schema on which to found his or her drawings. |
| There may be failure to comprehend how one may project space in three-dimensions upon a plane. | The student comprehends, and successfully depicts, three-dimensional space on a flat plane. |
| Manual skill may fail. | Manual skills and psycho-motor coordination are used appropriately in drawing. |
| There may be no artistic sense. | The student senses his or her artistic processes, progress, and completion while drawing. |
| Inability to draw may arise from a combination of various of these deficiencies. (Meumann 1912) | There are no blocks to a student's capacity and ability to draw. |

Drawings and paintings that were gathered as products of standardized art production tasks were analyzed by Lark-Horovitz and Norton and reported in 1959–60. Their work also fits into the proposed schema of naive to sophisticated stages as dimensions of a normally distributed concept of art talent. In their work, Lark-Horovitz and Norton (1959, 1960) reported ten factors that were used to categorize children's art products as "indifferent" or "remarkable." Their categories are roughly parallel to the Ns and SnS categories on the naive to sophisticated spectrum as shown in the following three examples:

| CHARACTERISTICS OF INDIFFERENT ART PRODUCTS (Ns) | CHARACTERISTICS OF REMARKABLE ART PRODUCTS (Sns) |
|---|---|
| *Grouping* | |
| Three or more figures or objects set apart at random or aligned without any other relationship except possibly that of content. | Three or more figures or objects interrelated by means of a balanced arrangement, color integration, or spatial cohesion. |

| CHARACTERISTICS OF INDIFFERENT ART PRODUCTS (Ns) | CHARACTERISTICS OF REMARKABLE ART PRODUCTS (Sns) |
|---|---|

*Resemblance to Style*

| | |
|---|---|
| Suggesting vaguely a style of painting or drawing that is "naturalistic" or "realistic" or contain "decorative elements." | Suggesting a specific style in painting (or drawing) such as "Impressionism" or some particular form of "Expressionism": e.g., definite distortions, abstraction, or color unification. |

*Portrayal of Shapes*

| | |
|---|---|
| Shapes clearly outlined and defined against light, paper ground, or colored areas or hesitating or ragged outline of shapes. | Indefinite outlining, blending into background or neighboring areas with the intention of a special pictorial effect. |
| | (Lark-Horovitz and Norton 1959, 1960) |

As descriptors of relatively naive or relatively sophisticated products of art tasks, these categoric descriptions can be further analyzed and used to generate similar descriptors that would elaborate each of the five naive to sophisticated stages proposed earlier. Categoric descriptors, verified by research, for introductory (NNs), rudimentary (Ns), intermediate (NsSn), advanced (Sn), and mastery level (SnS) stages of development, relative to various art media and forms of artistic expression, could be used to critique student art work as indicative of defined levels of attainment and evaluate student art work diagnostically, thereby defining specifiable learning needs. The research reported above, that defined various categories of artistic behaviors, seems to verify that artistic behaviors and characteristics of art production or studio products, can be defined specifically, categorized accurately, and evaluated to yield information about causes of inefficiency in drawing, as Meumann called them, or learning problems in art, as we would be more likely to call them today.

A naive to sophisticated scale, divided into seven categories, can be constructed to sort the results of standardized art tasks and the various categories of art talent will resemble standard deviations of intelligence on a normal distribution. The scale would look something like Figure 5. As with the study of giftedness, prior to such research as Terman's *Genetic Studies of Genius,* we are as unclear about the concept of art talent as early researchers were about intelligence. We need to test, through carefully de-

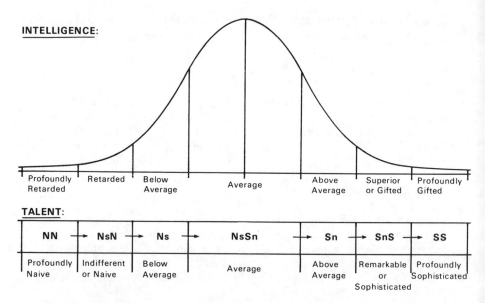

**FIGURE 5.** Distributions and categoric titles for groups of cases under portions of a distribution for Intelligence and Talent.

signed and executed research, each of the misconceptions, hypotheses, and assertions that have been stated in this chapter. We need to identify and study large numbers of subjects in order to learn more about those who have superior abilities in the visual arts. We need, further, to identify and study groups of subjects who, because of their characteristics, behaviors, and performances would enlighten our understanding of the entire spectrum of art talent. To study only the artistically superior student, without similar study of students with average and below average abilities, would lead away from clarifying and understanding the entire spectrum of art talent.

Terman's very early studies of what he called "stupid" and "bright" subjects (legitimate terms at that time) led, ultimately, to his monumental contribution to the science of intelligence testing. Educators need to define the concept of talent as it may be applied to all persons and to develop tools, devices, or experiences parallel to those of researchers who have created geometric leaps in our understanding of intelligence. It is possible, now, to begin to understand art talent in ways that it has never been understood before. The achievements of gifted children are truly remarkable;

the achievements of those with sophisticated talent in the arts are equally remarkable—but we must learn to recognize, guide, nurture, and reward them.

## SUMMARY AND CONCLUSIONS

In this chapter, the concept of art talent has been examined by presenting several popular misconceptions about students with superior abilities in art and by setting forth a new way to view the concept of talent in art. Misconceptions were countered with evidence from research or counter claims from persons who have studied artistically superior students. A new conception of talent in art was presented in which parallels were drawn between representation of the concept of intelligence on a normal distribution and representation of talent in art on a naive to sophisticated continuum.

Five popular misconceptions were presented and refuted: (1) art work by talented students is easy to recognize in a classroom, (2) above average intelligence is not a requirement for superior artistic performance, (3) children with superior artistic abilities are socially inept, physically immature, or emotionally unstable, (4) talented students need no instruction in art, they will learn on their own, and (5) every child is equally talented or, conversely, only a few children possess art talent.

Clarification of the concept of talent in art was presented through a series of related claims: (1) art talent, like intelligence, may be normally distributed, (2) differences in drawing skills and art behaviors of highly able and less able students are differences in degree and not in kind, (3) it is possible to categorize results of standardized artistic production, performance, and perception tasks on a naive to sophisticated scale, (4) a naive to sophisticated scale divided into seven categories can be used to sort the results of standardized art tasks and the categories will resemble standard deviations of intelligence on a normal distribution, (5) it is possible to construct visual exemplars and/or write verbal descriptions for each of the naive to sophisticated categories of talents in the arts, and (6) it is possible to sort art behaviors, products of standardized art tasks, and artistic performances into clearly illustrated or defined categories on a naive to sophisticated spectrum.

If these claims are verified by research, a new concept of talent in art can be constructed. In this new conception, every person has talent, but in varying degrees. Implications of this new concept of talent in art could effect teaching practices and art program design, especially for students with superior abilities in the arts.

A student at the Indiana University Summer Arts Institute is completing an acrylic painting while another observes her progress. Artistically talented students often critique each other's work in such informal situations. Such grouping of students with similar abilities provides supportive environments for learning in the arts. Photo by Bob Mosier.

PART 3 A PROGRAM STRUCTURE

*T*HE MARLAND REPORT (1972), the United States Office of Education, and the most recent federal legislation relative to gifted/talented children call for special educational programs appropriate to the needs of children who are identified as possessing superior abilities in intellectual, creative, specific academics, leadership, and the visual and performing arts. Such programs "require services or activities not ordinarily provided by the schools" (P L 95-561). In the visual arts, providing special services and activities is particularly difficult because most art programs in schools are wholly idiosyncratic. There are, therefore, few basic art programs from which policies for providing special services and activities can be created.

Renzulli (1977), Gallagher (1975), Newland (1976), Khatena (1982), Clark (1979), and others have all asserted that good gifted/talented educational programs must differ from general programs that are ordinarily provided by the schools. Too often, it is claimed, "many of the practices that typify programs for the gifted [and talented] are little more than a random collection of kits, games, puzzles, and artsy-craftsy activities and what we call differential education is basically a cosmetic reshuffling of many time-honored curricular practices that are essentially good for all students" (Renzulli 1977, p.i).

In order to avoid this accusation to a program for artistically talented students, it is necessary to establish unique program philosophy, purposes, goals, and structure that will guide all program decisions and define a special offering of services or activities not ordinarily provided by the schools. In order to do that, it is necessary to identify a basic program structure from which unique services and activities can be derived.

In 1983, we outlined a basic program structure for visual arts education that encompasses several curricular orientations (society-centered, child-centered, subject matter-centered) and curricular components (student, teacher, content, setting) (Clark and Zimmerman 1983f). Each of the components of student, teacher, content, and setting require adaptation from regular school programs to special services and activities appropriate for special programs for artistically talented students. How do such regular and special programs differ and how are they linked together?

## DEVELOPING A BASIC VISUAL ARTS
## PROGRAM STRUCTURE

School program planning has been viewed, traditionally, as representing three different orientations to schooling; these are society-centered, child-centered, and subject-matter-centered orientations. Many theorists (Lee and Lee 1950; Ragan 1953; Smith, Stanley, and Shores 1957; Tyler 1950) have discussed how curricula differ as a result of their focus upon society, the child, or subject matter. More contemporary expression of these traditional orientations, as art education constructs, are found in major publications authored and/or co-authored by Barkan, Chapman, Efland, Eisner, and Kern (Barkan and Chapman 1967; Chapman 1970; Efland 1970; Barkan, Chapman, and Kern 1970; Eisner 1972). Emphasizing one orientation and one set of goals does not preclude concern with the educational goals of other orientations. Improving society, helping each person achieve personal fulfillment, and transmitting the cultural heritage are generally recognized as goals that must be taught in order to create an enlightened citizenry (Chapman 1978). In a democratic society, all these goals and orientations must be given attention in adequate art education programs.

In a society-centered program, emphasis is upon meeting a community's social needs through learning social values and content derived from broad, social problems; learning activities evolve as outcomes of group needs and interests. The major role of the teacher is as coordinator and mediator of learning, guiding students in their efforts to meet a community's social needs. In an art program, emphasis would be upon helping students understand the role of art in society and the expression of social values through the arts.

In a child-centered program, expressed interests and needs of students determine content and structure for the curriculum; individual problem solving and self expression are the dominant methods. The major role of the teacher is to act as facilitator of the student's need for expression and as a mentor of the student's instruction. In an art program, emphasis would be upon helping each student express his or her personal needs and develop his or her capacities and abilities in art.

In a subject-matter-centered program, emphasis is based upon classified and organized disciplines of knowledge; learning activities emphasize methods, techniques, and findings within separate subject disciplines. The major role of the teacher is as programmer of content and instructor of knowledge, understandings, and skills. In an art program, emphasis would be upon perceptual-conceptual inquiry that would develop student capacities for skillful art production, criticism, and appreciation.

King and Brownell (1966) define curriculum as "a planned series of encounters between a student and some selection of communities of discourse" (pp. 121–22). Barkan (1963) defines the community of discourse that specifically delimits art education as the "learning experience in art" (p. 8). Steiner (1978) claims that properties of student, teacher, content, and setting need to be stated in order to establish adequate educational theory for school program planning. Based upon these definitions and constructs, we define general curriculum as a planned sequence of learning experiences, based on a particular content that includes student and teacher tasks and outcomes and that takes place in a specified educational setting. We define *art* curriculum, a subset of curriculum, as a planned sequence of learning experiences about art content that includes student and teacher tasks and outcomes and that takes place in an environment designed for art learning. To construct an adequate art program based upon this definition of curriculum, a complex of planned relationships among art content, student and teacher tasks and outcomes about art, and an educational setting that supports art learning must be specified.

We have established, in other places (Clark and Zimmerman 1978a, 1978b, 1981), that the important art content to be learned in an adequate art program should include knowledge, understandings, and skills about art history, art criticism, art production, and aesthetics. An adequate art program should also be concerned with a student's readiness for art learning and level of development, student art tasks and outcomes, and teacher's roles and methodologies related to appropriate learning experiences in art. The educational setting should be specified as an environment for art learning in the classroom, school, community, and society that includes the administrative climate, support mechanisms of the environment, and the immediate physical environment. The setting is also defined by additional factors of materials, equipment, other resources, and time available to teacher and students. These factors of components for an adequate art program are shown in Table 1. We believe that all decisions about these components should be meaningfully interrelated in order to facilitate successful learning experiences about art.

We originally presented this program structure as a basis for arguing that a good school art program would include *all* of the orientation/ component intersections and would, therefore, be complete. This argument also applies to unique programs for artistically talented students. It is important for *all* students to study various aspects of art that would contribute to improving society, achieving personal fulfillment, and knowing and understanding their cultural heritage.

TABLE 1

## FACTORS OF THREE EDUCATIONAL ORIENTATIONS AND FOUR CURRICULUM COMPONENTS AS A STRUCTURE FOR A COMPLETE VISUAL ARTS PROGRAM

| | STUDENT COMPONENT | TEACHER COMPONENT | CONTENT COMPONENT | SETTING COMPONENT |
|---|---|---|---|---|
| *Society-centered orientation* | Readiness and motivation for participation in art activities that result in social development and attainment of knowledges, understandings, and skills about art | Role as art coordinator and mediator based on a social interaction model<br><br>Strategies for social interaction toward the attainment of knowledge about art through society | Social orientation to selection of art content from art history, art criticism, art production, and aesthetics | Administrative arrangements, materials, and environments that facilitate social development and knowledge and skills about art |
| *Child-centered orientation* | Readiness and motivation for participation in art activities that result in personal development and attainment of knowledge, understandings, and skills about art | Role as art facilitator and mentor based on a personal sources model<br><br>Strategies for personal growth toward attainment of knowledge about art through the self | Personal orientation to selection of art content from art history, art criticism, art production, and aesthetics | Administrative arrangements, materials, and environments that facilitate personal development and knowledge and skills about art |
| *Subject-matter-centered orientation* | Readiness and motivation for participation in art activities that result in conceptual-perceptual development and attainment of knowledge, understandings, and skills about art | Role as art programmer and instructor based on an information processing model<br><br>Strategies for conceptual-perceptual inquiry toward attainment of knowledge, skills, and understandings about art | Information processing orientation to selection of art content from art history, art criticism, art production, and aesthetics | Administrative arrangements, materials, and environments that facilitate conceptual-perceptual development and knowledge and skills about art |

## DEVELOPING A SPECIAL VISUAL ARTS PROGRAM

Newland (1976) argues strongly for the need of program planners to establish a clearly defined philosophy as a basis for differentiating services to the gifted/talented. He also states that "it is not justifiable to think in terms of a philosophy unique to the gifted. . . . The general philosophy which should underlie all education would seem to hold . . . in the cases of all children . . . at most only a sharper delineation of the principles relevant the education of the gifted would appear to be needed" (pp. 118–19).

Most program orientations for artistically talented students will be viewed as expressions of society-centered, child-centered, and subject-matter-centered philosophies. According to Newland, however, such statements of philosophy should be made as clear and distinct as possible in order to avoid the ambiguities and generalizations often found in most general programs. In much the same way, decisions about student, teacher, content, and setting components need to be delineated as clearly as possible in order to define unique services and activities that set a special program for artistically talented students apart from the art program offered to other students in general programs.

Adaptations of the program structure just presented need to be made in planning and implementing a program for artistically talented students. The identification of this unique sub-group needs to be guided by decisions of program philosophy and goals. Their educational program, like that of other students, needs to accommodate to their unique readiness for art learning, level of development in art, and provide appropriate tasks and outcomes about art. Teachers of artistically talented students need to be aware that program philosophy and goals, or orientation, guide decisions about their roles and strategies appropriate to various aspects of the educational program. The content to be learned in a program for artistically talented students should be defined as accelerated and enriched learning experiences about art history, art criticism, art production, and aesthetics. Settings for special programs may be in schools, museums, community agencies or other places supportive to the education of artistically talented students. These adaptations are shown in Table 2.

To respond to these needs, in 1978 we organized and implemented the Indiana University Summer Arts Institute that integrates student, teacher, content, and setting components (Clark and Zimmerman 1983d, 1983e). This program is designed to provide unique learning opportunities for students in the seventh through tenth grades who are seriously interested in intensive study of the visual arts, along with music, dance, and drama. Participants are required to meet specific criteria and be nominated by pro-

TABLE 2

## ADAPTATIONS FOR SPECIAL PROGRAMS

| Artistically Talented Student | Teacher of Artistically Talented Students | Content for Artistically Talented Students | Settings for Artistically Talented Students |
|---|---|---|---|
| Readiness for art learning.<br><br>Level of development in art.<br><br>Appropriate tasks and outcomes about art. | Role in learning experiences about art appropriate to artistically talented students.<br><br>Teaching strategies related to art learning for artistically talented students. | Accelerated and enriched learning experiences about art history, art criticism, art production, and aesthetics. | School, community and society as environments for art learning for artistically talented students. |

fessionals in their schools. For two weeks, during midsummer, 65 selected participants from throughout Indiana and adjoining states attend this institute. Most participants live in a campus dormitory; a few commute to the Indiana University campus from the local community. The I. U. Summer Arts Institute provides many opportunities to explore and extend participants' talents and abilities in a university environment. In addition to attending major painting, drawing, sculpture, and computer graphics classes, participants also select visual arts, music, dance, and drama electives. Institute faculty, from the I.U. Departments of art education, fine arts, theater, music, and dance, are selected on the basis of their background and experience. Students are also offered organized recreational activities and evening programs designed to meet their particular interests and needs as artistically talented students.

Nomination criteria for this program are: (1) high interest in one or several of the arts, (2) successful experience in one or several of the visual arts, (3) high motivation and self-confidence in one or several of the visual arts, (4) achievement tests scores at least two grades higher than the student's present grade, (5) measured, above-average intelligence, (6) or placement in a local gifted and talented school program. Students must be nominated by two or more of the following persons: a principal, counselor, arts specialist, or teacher to participate in the I.U. Summer Arts Institute.

Students who study silkscreening at the Indiana University Summer Arts Institute begin by examining works of artists and do a series of interpretations of such works. This silkscreen print, by a seventh grader who had never silkscreened before, is derived from a Picasso painting and demonstrates the student's individual interpretation. Photo by Indiana University AV Services.

A curriculum for high ability art students must differ from that offered to average or below average students. Superior students in the visual arts should receive more opportunities for in-depth learning experiences than are typically offered in schools. Teachers with experience in working with talented art students and with expertise in an art form can help such students maximize their potential. Students benefit from related series of learning experiences in one media or about one major skill or concept. They can be led to experience sophisticated inquiry based on role models of the artist, art critic, art historian, or aesthetician. As in the I.U. Summer Arts Institute, their learning activities should be clearly based upon and derived from study of art works by artists and writings by art critics, art historians, and aestheticians (Clark and Zimmerman 1978a, 1981). A curriculum for artistically talented students also should be more demanding and challenging, should be accelerated in pace and amount of material to be learned, and should establish higher levels of achievement that demand the greatest degree of independent activities and learning as possible. These goals are best met by bringing artistically talented students together for all or part of their school day or in special programs, such as the I.U. Summer Arts Institute, that differ from the general visual arts programs offered in the schools. Many I.U. Summer Arts Institute participants comment about the delight they have felt by their interactions with a group of students "like themselves" and the challenges they have faced when working with others as equally talented as themselves. This awareness, and pressure, is positive and results in a striving to excellence that is not always present in regular school programs.

In the following chapters, suggested adaptations are discussed in detail and expanded to include historical backgrounds, contemporary applications, current research and implementations and recommendations for the creation and support of programs for artistically talented students. In addition, suggestions for needed research are offered relative to each program component.

In Chapters 2 through 5, the following issues are discussed: identifying artistically talented students, role of the teacher for artistically talented students, curriculum content for artistically talented students, educational settings and administrative arrangements for artistically talented students, and a summary and recommendations for contemporary programs. Thus, the four program components that should be adapted in order to provide services and activities not ordinarily provided by the schools are clarified and amplified.

This crayon drawing by a kindergarten girl shows an unusual sense of balance, use of space, and decorative qualities for a child of her age. The rhythm, created by repetition and spacing, and the sensitive line qualities of this delightful drawing indicate potential talent if the child continues to do art work of similar quality. Photo by Indiana University AV Services.

PART I  REVIEW OF IDENTIFICATION INQUIRY
AND RESEARCH

> The grown-up's response . . . was to advise me
> to lay aside my drawings . . . and devote myself instead
> to geography, history, arithmetic, and grammar. That is
> why, at the age of six, I gave up what might have been
> a magnificent career as a painter. . . . Grown-ups never
> understand anything by themselves, and it is tiresome for
> children to be always and forever explaining things to
> them.                            (De Saint-Exupéry 1943, p. 8)

*J*T IS MORE THAN FORTY YEARS since De Saint-Exupéry wrote *The Little Prince.* Finally, grown-ups are beginning to understand the needs of artistically talented students by identifying them and by establishing programs that encourage using pencils to draw, as an important educational goal, rather than only using them to solve arithmetic problems. For more than fifty years, however, education for gifted / talented students has over emphasized "hard" subject matters and academic programs and focused attention upon students whose abilities are academically and intellectually superior (Passow 1979). One result has been "neglect of the arts, both fine and practical, in the effort to shore up the 'academic' part of the curriculum" (Gold 1965, p. 254.).

The term "talented" has become disassociated from specific reference to demonstrated, superior abilities in the arts. In 1958, Getzels and Jackson called attention to the need to differentiate between definitions of academically gifted, talented, and creative children. Getzels and Jackson did not equate creativity with artistic talent. Their research identified students with creative abilities in traditional academic subjects rather than in the arts. Getzels' and Jacksons' research was made possible because intelligence and creativity were defined as specific observable behaviors. This capability to test and quantify operationally defined behaviors on a standardized test is a major factor underlying the fifty-year over emphasis upon *academic* education for gifted and talented students.

A number of people have acknowledged that "intelligence as a measurable capacity must . . . be defined as the capacity to do well on an intelligence test" (Boring 1923, p. 35). Likewise, the operational definition of creativity is "what creativity tests measure" (Gallagher 1975, p. 55). As a result, IQ is commonly defined as the degree of successful performance on an individually administered IQ test, such as the Stanford-Binet or WISC. Creativity is commonly defined as the degree of successful performance on a standardized test of creativity, such as the Torrance Tests of Creativity (Torrance 1966, 1974). Art talent as a construct separate from intelligence or creativity, has not been operationally defined as a performance level on a standardized test (Salome 1974). As a result, few researchers have devoted attention to studying talented children who have superior abilities in the visual arts. Talent, as a term, has been used, instead, to mean gifted, creative, or academic superiority in other school subjects than art.


## RECENT LEGISLATION FOR STUDENTS
## WITH SUPERIOR ABILITIES IN THE VISUAL ARTS

The attitude of the grown-ups in *The Little Prince,* who advised the child to discard his drawings and devote himself to more important subjects, belittled the child's superior abilities in the visual arts and misdirected the child's art talent. Many other children have had adults react to their art work in the same way. It was only as recently as 1972 that artistically talented children were acknowledged by the federal government as a population worthy of attention within schools. In 1972, Sidney Marland was U.S. Commissioner of Education when the Marland Report identified children capable of high performance in the visual and performing arts as a subgroup of gifted and talented students. The Marland Report contributed greatly to implementation of The Special Projects Act of 1975 (PL 93-380) and The Gifted and Talented Children's Education Act as part of Public Law 95-561. The following statement is found in Section 902 of the current Gifted and Talented Children's Act of 1978:

> For the purpose of this legislation, the term "gifted and talented" means children and whenever applicable, youth, who are identified at the preschool, elementary or secondary level as possessing demonstrated or potential abilities which give evidence of high performance responsibility in areas such as intellectual, creative, specific academics, or leadership abilities or in the performing, and visual arts and who by reason thereof, require services or activities not ordinarily provided by the school.

In greater detail, categories of giftedness from the Gifted and Talented Children's Act of 1978 are:

1. *General intellectual ability* — Across the board superiority in academics; consistently superior scores on many appropriate standardized tests; demonstration of advanced skills, imaginative insight, and intense interest and involvement.
2. *Specific academic aptitude* — Consistently demonstrated superiority in a specific academic area.
3. *Creative and/or productive thinking* — Superiority in original, imaginative thought processes, with fluency of (idea) production.
4. *Leadership ability* — Employs a highly developed moral and/or ethical network in social interaction, has ability to move individuals successfully through a task.
5. *Visual or performing arts* — Demonstrated superior abilities in dance, theatre, creative writing, the arts, etc..

This legislation has offered art educators and art teachers, throughout the country, a major opportunity to implement research and develop programs to meet the needs of public school students with superior abilities in the visual arts. Neither the Marland Report nor Public Law 95-561, however, offers an operational definition of talent in the visual arts.

## SEVENTY YEARS OF INQUIRY

Historically, study of public school children with superior abilities in the visual arts is now at a similar stage as study of gifted children with superior intellectual abilities was in the 1920s. Researchers in several countries were involved in inquiry about giftedness at that time, but there had not yet been a comprehensive development of ideas and research findings to unify these inquiries. As a result of Terman's leadership of a comprehensive, longitudinal study of over a thousand gifted children, first published in 1925, theoretical bases and operational constructs were established that set the stage for future inquiry about giftedness (Guilford 1967). Prior to Terman's research, knowledge about giftedness had been based upon inferences and isolated studies of small groups of gifted children.

Today, the study of students with superior abilities in the visual arts is based largely upon stated inferences and idiosyncratic, isolated research about individuals and small groups of subjects. The following chronological survey will be limited to presenting and summarizing findings from seventy years of diverse inquiry by independent researchers about identification of elementary and secondary students with superior abilities in the visual arts. Studies of adult populations, including college students, will not be reported because such groups often consist of individuals who have already demonstrated art talent and are recognized as having superior abilities in the visual arts. From the early 1900s through the 1940s, there were a number of research studies that focused upon behaviors of students with superior abilities in the visual arts and characteristics of their art work.

## RESEARCH FROM 1900 TO 1949

In the early 1900s, a number of German researchers were among the first to initiate inquiry about children's drawing talent and the effects of heredity and environment upon drawing abilities. Among these were Kerschensteiner (1905), Kik (1908), and Meumann (1912, 1914). Kerschensteiner and Kik each studied the development of drawing in children and, in doing so, they identified a small number of highly talented children. They then studied these highly talented children through case study methods. Their case study methodology was an important contribution although they did not reach any conclusions about the prediction of drawing talent.

In 1912, Meumann described several factors that caused an inability to draw well. His conclusions from his teaching, were based upon observed differences between highly able and less able groups of students. In this very early research, he recognized that factors he identified described differences in degree between individuals. He classified these factors as talent related, practice related, or related to a combination of talent and practice. Research in the United States followed soon after these efforts.

Ayer studied groups of students, using a laboratory procedure, and analyzed their modes of drawing in progress, types of drawing, school achievement, and verbal abilities of recall and description (1916). In 1916, he published a report in which he attempted to differentiate between highly able and less able students on different measures of drawing ability and other characteristics.

Manuel (1919a, 1919b) reported his study of the drawing abilities of students selected for participation in a study of gifted children in Urbana, Illinois. He reported observations of students, who were talented in drawing, in relationship to psychophysical characteristics general intelligence, linguistic ability, motor ability, and handwriting ability.

In 1923, Hollingworth studied variables that seemed to be closely related to the ability to draw and wrote that "At present, we have no means of gauging talent in drawing except by grading a finished product on a scale of drawings . . . [though] such a means does not always separate talent from training" (p. 146). She also claimed that general intelligence conditions the ability to do art work. Three years later, Hollingworth (1926) studied the relationship between intelligence and the abilities of students to make various kinds of drawings. Fritz, in 1930, also reported a close relationship between general mental ability and performance on a drawing test and described characteristics of talented students.

Partially as a result of their early work in the testing of art and music abilities, Meier and Seashore claimed to be able to differentiate between children with superior abilities in the arts and those who were not superior (Meier and Seashore 1930; Meier 1939). The characteristics they identified were manual skill, energy, aesthetic intelligence, perceptual facility, and creative imagination. These characteristics were to be found in all children, they claimed, but to a higher degree in talented children. Klar and Winslow, in 1933, suggested that teachers use various tests to help identify students with superior abilities in visual arts. Tests he suggested were the Goodenough Drawing Scale, The McCarty Drawing Scale, the Kline-Carey Drawing Scale, the Lewerenz Test of Fundamental Abilities in the Visual Arts, the Meier Seashore Art Judgement Test, and the McAdory Art Test.

Two studies of elementary and high school students, reported in 1936, described relationships between students with superior art abilities and characteristics of their art work, motor control, and intelligence. Cane (1936) described differences in quality of line, design and organization, and imaginative and dynamic qualities of elementary students' art work, as well as differences in students' motor development as indicators of giftedness in art. Tiebout and Meier (1936) found similarities between intellectual capacities of high school students, who were described as superior in art, and practicing artists.

As early as 1933, under the leadership of Munro (1956), one of the single, most important studies of students' art abilities was begun at the Cleveland Museum of Art. Over a number of years, thirteen hundred students were involved in performing on a series of standardized tasks of *The Seven Drawing Test*. This test was administered to all children participating in the Museum's Saturday Art Classes as well as to children in Cleveland's public schools. On the basis of results of performance on these standardized tasks, children were grouped into "special" and "average" classes. Special classes were advanced, museum classes for talented students; average classes were composed of public school and museum students whose test performance was described as average. *The Seven Drawing Test* included drawing from memory, copying, and drawing from imagination. Later development of aesthetic response tasks and devices for recording and analyzing children's work over specified periods of time made it possible for more factors to be studied and reported. Reports about the Cleveland studies focused upon task performance and other characteristics that differentiated average and special groups of students. Criteria that were used to describe these differences included (1) characteristics of drawings such as color, line, shape, organization, technique, media, and content, (2) types of drawings, either realistic or schematic, (3) tendencies to copy and to express and experience phenomena visually, (4) intelligence and rates of learning, (5) abilities to defend aesthetic preferences and objectify responses to art work, and (6) degree of interest and desire to produce art (Lark-Horovitz 1937, 1941; Lark-Horovitz, Barnhardt, and Sills 1939; Munro, Lark-Horovitz, and Barnhardt 1956; Lark-Horovitz, Lewis, and Luca 1967). All factors reported for the Cleveland Studies were described as differences in degree, between averages and specials, and not as isolated characteristics of the special groups.

## RESEARCH FROM 1950 TO 1970

There was a dramatic rise, during the 1950s and early 1960s, in federal support for educational research and an increased interest in the study of giftedness and creativity as research constructs. Support and interest in each of these efforts decreased during the late 1960s and 1970s (Goodlad 1966; Tannenbaum 1979). The 1954 Supreme Court decision to desegregate public schools started an educational movement that placed the cause of disadvantaged children as a top priority for federal, state, and local funding. In the 1960s and 1970s, there was "a deep valley of neglect of gifted and talented education in which the public fixed its attention more eagerly on the low functioning, poorly motivated, and socially handicapped children in our schools" (Tannenbaum 1979, p. 5). Despite this neglect, many independent researchers continued to investigate characteristics of students with superior abilities in the visual arts during the 1960s and 1970s.

An important identification and classification technique for identifying talented students was developed during the 1950s. *The work-sample technique* evolved from desire of researchers to do structured observations of students' art work. Kough and DeHaan (1955) suggested that a portfolio of art work be kept for individual students and that the contents be evaluated by outside experts to identify students with superior abilities. Havighurst, Stivers, and DeHaan (1955) discussed how nonstandardized art tasks could be screened and evaluated by outside experts. Further evolution of the work-sample technique required evaluation by standardized rather than idiosyncratic art tasks. As conditions for art tasks became more controlled, criteria for judging art products were clarified and judges were trained to use predetermined criteria to identify students' art work that indicated superior abilities in the visual arts (DeHaan 1957; Witty, Conant, and Strang 1959; Inglehart 1960).

During the 1950s, a number of researchers who used various forms of the work-sample technique to identify artistically talented students, reported differences on similar characteristics as those that had been reported for the Cleveland Studies. For example, Kough and DeHaan (1955) distinguished talented students in the visual arts by the content, depth, proportion, originality of expression, uses of media, and visual expression in their art work, and by their ability to respond to works of art. Kough and De-Haan (1955), Conant and Randall (1959), and Inglehart (1960) stressed, as had reports of the Cleveland Studies, the roles of interest, desire, persistence, and self-motivation to do art work as important characteristics that could be used to identify students with potential for high achievement in the visual arts.

Lark-Horovitz and Norton (1959, 1960) reported further work based upon the original Cleveland Studies. They identified ten factors that they used to characterize children's art work as "remarkable" or "indifferent." Remarkable art work showed evidence of superior ability in the visual arts; the factors studied were representation, color, grouping, symmetry, shape, style, motion, media, area, and line. A few years previously, Lindstrom (1957) had claimed that gifted students in the visual arts could be identified by factors of perception of the world, ability to structure parts into wholes, depth of appreciation, readiness to respond to new experiences, and reactions to frustrating experiences.

In the fourth edition of *Creative and Mental Growth,* published in 1964, Lowenfeld and Brittain described factors that distinguished gifted from average children; these included imagination, expression, use of media, subject matter, and personal involvement. In 1966, Hildreth also discussed differences between superior and average art students; factors she reported included interest in art, ambition for an art career, energy level, and previous knowledge about art. Yochim (1967) studied 6,000 paintings by elementary and secondary students over a period of fifteen years and reported her findings in 1967. She claimed that superior art students also performed well in science, social studies, language arts, mathematics, and other highly disciplined areas of the curriculum.

Questions were raised in the early 1960s about using standardized measures and tests to identify superior art students. Waddell claimed that excellence in art emerges only in adulthood and that "it is impossible to determine specific giftedness at an early age" (1960, pp. 69–70.) Brittain (1961) questioned the use of standardized art tests because they become dated soon after their publication and are only valid as they reflect the preferences and correct responses determined by the test designer. Zeigfeld (1961) also questioned whether objective measurement of art talent was possible. Lowenfeld and Brittain (1964) challenged whether intelligence tests could be used, at all, to identify students with superior abilities in the visual arts. This claim was consistent with their belief that "every child is potentially gifted" (Lowenfeld & Brittain 1964, p. 393).

In their second edition of *Children and Their Art,* Gaitskill and Hurwitz (1970) summarized previously identified factors that had been used by researchers to select talented children. These factors were catagorized as intelligence, skill, and uniqueness of art production. Yet, similar concerns about identification of talented students as those voiced in the 1950s and 1960s were repeated in the early 1970s and remain major identification problems today. In 1973, Ashley noted, as Hollingworth had in 1923, that talent is widespread among students and that there are *no* satisfactory tests available for identifying students with superior talent in the fine arts. She reiterated the value of using work-sample products and called, again, for judgment of work-samples by outside experts.

## RESEARCH FROM 1971 TO PRESENT

A new sensitivity to the relationship between intelligence and talent emerged in the early 1970s. During the late 1950s and through most of the 1960s, educational efforts focussed upon programs designed for disadvantaged students. Two effects of these efforts were to challenge or discontinue the use of intelligence tests in identification and grouping of children in special classes. Another effect of these efforts was that all children were viewed as potentially gifted, talented, or creative. As a result, special classes for gifted or talented students became suspect and almost disappeared. A reaction emerged during the early 1970s favoring equal attention to gifted education rather than exclusive attention to the education of disadvantaged students. One result has been that "Attention to individual competencies among the handicapped has dramatized the need to individualize education, with every child receiving a fair share of what is uniquely appropriate for him" (Tannenbaum 1979, p. 26).

Renewed interest in a positive correlation between intelligence and talent of all kinds reflected earlier claims that Hollingworth and others had made since 1923. Schubert concluded, in 1973, that intelligence controls the development of art abilities but does not insure such development. Vernon, Adamson, and Vernon, in 1977, claimed that most children with high IQs are talented and that most talented children also have high IQs. They noted, however, that children with special talents might not score as high on intelligence tests as academically talented children. These claims had been verified in an earlier, but little publicized, research. Pegnato and Birch (1959) found that students identified as gifted by art and music teachers were also identified as gifted by their performance on at least two other screening devices unrelated to art or music. Inglehart (1960) and Hoyle and Wilks (1975) have speculated that a relatively high level of IQ, about 120 + , is a prerequisite for high achievement in specific areas of talent, including talent in the arts.

Questions about the correlation of intelligence and art ability are raised by examination of unique cases such as Gottfried Mind, Nadia, and Richard Wawro. These three cases of exceptional children with outstanding art abilities are enigmas and at this time unexplainable. In the past, terms such as "idiot savant" or "talented aments" have been used though these terms are often inappropriate and are too broad to be applied to individual cases. Gottfried Mind, born in Berne Switzerland in 1768, was considered a cretin and imbecile. He showed considerable talent at an early age for drawing and, in later life, his realistic drawings and paintings made him famous throughout Europe (Tredgold 1937). Selfe (1977) reports the case of Nadia, an autistic child, born in England, with very limited verbal skills who was able to make highly sensitive, sophisticated drawings at the age of three. Her exceptional drawing ability diminished as she attended school and began to develop social and verbal skills. Nadia produced extraordinary drawings again when she reached adolescence (Winner 1982). Richard Wawro was diagnosed as legally blind, severely retarded, and having other multiple handicaps. Despite these limitations he has been, from the age of three, able to create unique, realistic drawings with oil crayons (Becker 1983).

Such cases as these confound attempts to explain relationships between intelligence and art abilities. There are many theories that attempt to explain phenomenal drawing ability in exceptional children. The problem of misdiagnosis and inability to measure the true skills and abilities of persons with special communication and other handicaps are some explanations that have been suggested (Selfe 1977).

There are also children who apparently demonstrate art skills and abilities at superior levels whose achievement in other subject matters is at or below average. Such children occur somewhat frequently just as there are similar children whose mathematical or language skills may far exceed their achievement in other subjects. Again, explanation of outstanding skills and abilities in one area disproportionate to achievement in other areas has been discussed but not fully explained by others. Jones (1926) discusses persistence in a preferred activity, and the ignoring of other activities, as a possible explanation. Jaensch (1930) reports his study of subjects with eidetic memory as a possible explanation for superior development of a single ability. Winner (1982) believes that Nadia probably possessed an "innate, probably neurological proclivity in the visual arts" (p. 188) and that her conceptual deficiency allowed her to create astonishing works of art at a very early age. Educators may find Morgan's (1936) explanation the most disturbing. He claims that miseducation, resulting in special nurturance of a peculiar interest or talent, to the exclusion of other subjects, may result from nurturing and rewarding a child in only one area of achievement. Selfe (1977) notes that research about children whose art skills and abilities far exceed abilities in other areas was an interest in the 1920s and 1930s and is generally lacking today.

There have been several cautions expressed about early identification of artistically talented students. Several researchers have claimed that early display of artistic talent may not persist into adulthood and that mature artistic talent may not, for various reasons, be apparent until adulthood (Hoyle and Wilks 1975; Vernon, Adamson, and Vernon 1977; Waddell 1960).

The Cleveland Studies categorized art students by their performance on a series of drawing tasks. Similar sets of tasks have been designed by other researchers seeking to identify children with superior abilities in the visual arts. Witty, Conant, and Strang (1959) reported early use of the work sample technique in 1959. More recent adaptations of the work sample technique have added predetermined criteria for the judging of work samples collected from assigning the same art task to a group of students. Superior performance on such standardized tasks were used in Norwalk, Connecticut (Doob 1975) and Poulsbo, Washington (Peterson 1977) to select a small percentage of highly talented students to participate in special programs in the visual arts. Similar criteria were used in both programs to judge art products and student behaviors; these criteria included originality, flexibility, complexity, skill, motivation, and perseverance.

A more recent approach to identification of artistically superior students is to assemble a list of characteristics and behaviors common to talented students and to select students who demonstrate the greatest number of these characteristics. Actual artistic performance on specific art tasks is not required by this technique and it may, therefore, be used to identify potentially talented students or students who, though capable, may not be performing at a superior level. A major summary of such lists of characteristics, reported by Luca and Allen in 1974, includes characteristics under four major headings: interest in art, learning behaviors, social behaviors, and performance patterns.

Wilson and Wilson, have reported many case studies of children who appear to display a specific type of talent in the visual arts. Their subjects, junior and senior high school students who draw highly elaborated "visual narratives," were described by behavior characteristics and observable characteristics of their drawings. Behavior characteristics, cited by the Wilsons, include a fascination for visual things, an encyclopedic visual memory, and a drive to create numerous visual images in the form of highly complex visual narratives. These visual narratives also display many visual characteristics and artistic devices used by comic book artists. The Wilsons claimed that extensive production of visual narratives, by students, leads to an intuitive development of individual style and serves as a transition to mature artistic efforts.

## SUMMARY AND CONCLUSIONS

In this review of research, from 1912 to the present, many characteristics that were used to identify elementary and secondary students with superior abilities in the visual arts have been presented. Many issues, relative to the identification of students with superior abilities in the visual arts have also been raised and remain unresolved.

A major issue, recurrent in the past history of inquiry about talented children, is the relationship between IQ and talent and specifically between IQ and superior ability in the visual arts. The question of whether scores on an IQ test are positively related to superior abilities in the visual arts has been partly answered by research, but is still a matter of controversy among art educators. Measurement capability at this time is insufficient to provide evidence for the explanation of superior art skills and abilities in unique and exceptional cases as well as in the general population. Another aspect of this IQ/art talent issue is whether talent in the visual arts can or should be measured by standardized tests.

An issue that still deserves more analysis and attention, though it has been reported for more than sixty years, is the recurrent finding that differences in the art work of less able, able, and highly able children differs only in degree, not in kind. In other words, specific characteristics can be observed in the art work of all children, but that only qualitative differences in these characteristics differentiate between the art work of average, less able, and talented children. This finding has been claimed many times, but it has not been analyzed for implications to accurate identification of children with superior abilities in the visual arts.

Two common but different indices for identifying talented students has been used over the past eighty years. One means is to observe characteristics of the drawings of talented students, the other is to observe various general characteristics of talented students. From these observations, lists of characteristics of drawings and behavior characteristics of talented students have been formulated. These two identification indices have been used separately and together. Most recent recommendations, by art educators concerned with the education of artistically talented students, have been for simultaneous use of both indices as corroborative evidence of talent. The issue that is raised is that neither index has been proven to be more effective or efficient than the other, nor has their simultaneous use been proven exhaustive as an identification device.

The work-sample technique of identification, based upon characteristics of student art work, has evolved throughout the history of inquiry about students with superior abilities in the visual arts. As with other tests of art talent, the work-sample technique had limited successes and generalizability in its earlier forms. Attempts have been made to impose standardization of art tasks and standardized criteria of judgement as conditions of use of the work-sample technique. However, the work-sample technique is, at this time, still a local, idiosyncratic device that remains in need of definition and standardization in a valid and reliable form that would be acceptable to art educators throughout the country.

Another intriguing, and wholly unresolved, issue relates to the maturation and persistence of talent in the visual arts. Three basic questions relate to this issue: (1) how early can art talent be identified, (2) if identified early, does art talent persist into adulthood, and (3) does art talent only emerge in adulthood? Each of these questions has been addressed, yet no resolution has emerged from past research.

Finally, the inquiry reported in this review has, obviously, produced a long list of characteristics that have been at one time or another, used to identify students with superior abilities in the visual arts. The accumulative list is unwieldly and inefficient for generalized use in identification procedures. It has produced, also, contradictory claims and inconsistent findings that must be resolved in the pursuit of effective identification and education of talented children. There has not been a critical evaluation of the many, specific characteristics that could be used to create an efficient and effective index that art teachers and program supervisors could use for identification of students with superior abilities in the visual arts. Implications of this historical review of inquiry about children with superior abilities in the visual arts and of emergent issues related to this inquiry, relative to programs in today's public schools, will be discussed more fully in Parts 2 and 3 of this chapter.

This high school student is doing a life drawing at the Boston University Summer School of the Arts. The student appears to display confidence with the charcoal, has used an experimental variety of lines, and shows an understanding of the interrelationship of the parts of the figure he is observing. Observing such process behaviors helps to identify artistically talented students. Photo by Boston University Photo Service.

## PART 2 STUDENT CHARACTERISTICS

*I*N THE PREVIOUS PART, much information from past research and inquiry was presented about identifying students who are talented in the visual arts. Although a large body of information is now available, the findings are confusing because they have been generated from many, different researchers and at many, different times. Researchers have often worked in isolation from other researchers interested in similar problems. Findings generated at different periods of time are reflective of different methodologies, research tools, and emphases upon different research questions. When research about aspects of a specific problem is conducted in isolation, or at different periods of time, the resulting claims are often contradictory and inconsistent to one another.

In this chapter, we will report specific claims about characteristics of art products and observable behaviors of students with superior abilities in the visual arts. All claims from the literature we have reviewed will be reported without attempting to reconcile or resolve, at this time, the apparent contradictions and inconsistencies that appear. Specific claims about characteristics of artistically talented students and their art work will be outlined. Each claim will be referenced to its origins by the names of person(s) who reported each claim and the date reported.

The outline is divided into categories that summarize research and inquiry about characteristics of students with superior abilities in the visual arts. The two largest categories are observable characteristics of art products and observable behaviors of students. The category of product characteristics refers to observable characteristics of art products and is divided into subcategories of compositional arrangement, elements and principles, subject matter, art making skills, and art making techniques. The category of observable behaviors of students with superior abilities in the visual arts is subdivided into predispositional behaviors and observable process behaviors. Predispositional behaviors are behaviors that are observable in a student, independent of the creation of an art product and include categories of generalized behaviors, art specific behaviors, art talent/IQ correlation behaviors, and art talent/subject matter correlation behaviors. Observable process behaviors are observable behaviors of students during the processes of making or criticizing art.

This tempera painting, by a second grade girl, demonstrates the use of three or more objects integrated as a balanced arrangement. The use of varied sizes, overlapping, placement of objects, and the textured background all show an unusual sophistication for a second grade student. Photo by Indiana University AV Services.

I. Observable characteristics of art products of students with superior abilities in the visual arts

    A. Compositional arrangement

        1. Skillful composition (Cane 1936; Lark-Horovitz 1941; Munro 1956; Lark-Horovitz, Lewis, and Luca 1967; Gaitskell and Hurwitz 1970; Luca and Allen 1974)

        2. Designs are complete and coherent (Cane 1936; Lark-Horovitz 1941; Munro 1956; Lark-Horovitz, Lewis, and Luca, 1967; Gaitskell and Hurwitz 1970; Luca and Allen 1974)

        3. Purposeful, asymmetrical arrangement with stability in irregular placement (Lark-Horovitz and Norton 1959–60)

        4. Three or more objects integrated by a balanced arrangement (Lark-Horovitz and Norton 1959–60)

        5. Complex composition (Munro 1956; Doob 1975)

        6. Elaboration and depiction of details (Conant and Randall 1959; Luca and Allen 1974)

    B. Elements and principles

        1. Well-organized colors, deliberate brilliancy and contrast, subtle blending of colors (Lark-Horovitz 1941; Kough and DeHaan 1955; Munro 1956; Lark-Horovitz, Lewis, and Luca 1967)

        2. Decisive and bold use of line, clarity of outline, subtle use of line (Cane 1936, Kough and DeHaan 1955; Munro 1956)

        3. Accurate depiction of light and shadow (Kough and DeHaan 1955)

        4. Intentional use of indefinite shapes, hazy outlines, shapes blend into background (Lark-Horovitz and Norton 1959–60)

        5. Excellence in many aspects of art including color, form, grouping, movement (Lark-Horovitz, Lewis, and Luca 1967)

    C. Subject matter

        1. Specializes in one subject matter (Lowenfeld and Brittain 1964; Lark-Horovitz, Lewis, and Luca 1967; Luca and Allen 1974)

        2. Draws a wide variety of things (Kough and DeHaan 1955)

        3. Sometimes copies to acquire technique (Lark-Horovitz and Norton 1959–60; Lark-Horovitz, Lewis, and Luca 1967)

        4. Adept at depiction of movement (Lark-Horovitz, Lewis, and Luca 1967; Wilson and Wilson 1976)

This crayon drawing of a cat, by a first grade boy, demonstrates use of hazy outline and shapes that blend into the background to express the student's feelings about his pet cat. The proportions, details, and placement of the subject are unusual for a first-grade student. Photo by Indiana University AV Services.

This true-to-appearance pencil drawing, by a seventh-grade girl, demonstrates accurate depiction of depth, light and shadow, excellent proportions, and the use of subtle and clear pencil lines to effectively depict the sleeping cat. Obviously based upon sophisticated observations, the accuracy yet expressiveness of the drawing indicates unusual talent. Photo by Indiana University AV Services.

5. Uses personal experiences and feelings as subject matter (Kough and DeHaan 1955; Laycock 1957; Lowenfeld and Brittain 1964)

D. Art-making skills

1. True-to-appearance representation (Munro 1956; Lark-Horovitz and Norton 1959–60)

2. Accurate depiction of depth by perspective (Kough and DeHaan 1955)

3. Use of good proportion (Kough and DeHaan 1955)

4. Schematic and expressive representation (schematic-decorative) (Munro 1956)

5. Effective use of media (Lark-Horovitz and Norton 1959–60)

6. May lack sufficient technical skills to represent mature talent (Waddell 1960; Hoyle and Wilks 1975; Vernon, Adamson, and Vernon 1977)

7. Products show obvious talent and artistic expression (Munro 1956; Havighurst 1958; Conant and Randall 1959; Gaitskell and Hurwitz 1970; Doob 1975; Peterson 1977)

E. Art-making techniques

1. Areas treated to display boldness, blending, gradation, and textures (Lark-Horovitz and Norton 1959–60)

2. Visual narratives used for self-expression and as a basis for mature art expression (Ayer 1916; Wilson and Wilson 1976)

    a. predominant vertical lines and forms

    b. maximum black and white contrast

    c. rapid zig-zag movement

    d. shifting view points

    e. literal action

    f. different sized frames

    g. heavy inking and cross-hatching

    h. maximum use of tools and media

3. Uses smaller paper (Lark-Horovitz 1941)

II. Observable behaviors of students with superior abilities in the visual arts

A. Predispositional behaviors

1. Generalized predispositional behaviors

    a. superior manual skill and good muscular control (Meier 1930; Cane 1936; Luca and Allen 1974)

b. independence of ideas and ability to experience events from multiple points of view (Luca and Allen 1974)

c. adherence to rules and regulations and routine study (Luca and Allen 1974)

d. relative freedom from ordinary frustration (Lindstrom 1957)

e. highly individualized differences in psychological characteristics (Manual 1919; Ziegfeld 1961; Lowenfeld and Brittain 1964; Luca and Allen 1974)

f. superior energy level and rapid turnover of thoughts (Fritz 1930; Meier 1930; Hildreth 1966; Luca and Allen 1974)

g. desire to work alone (Luca and Allen 1974)

h. compulsion to organize to satisfy desire for precision and clarity (Luca and Allen 1974)

i. highly adaptable in thought and activity (Luca and Allen 1974)

j. high potential for leadership due to fluency of ideas offered in a group (Fritz 1930; Luca and Allen 1974)

k. good concentration and flexibility in adaptation of knowledge (Luca and Allen 1974)

2. Art-specific predispositional behaviors

a. dynamic and intuitive quality of imagination (Meier 1930; Cane 1936; Munro 1956; Lowenfeld and Brittain 1964; Luca and Allen 1974; Wilson and Wilson 1976)

b. unusual penchant for visual imagery and fantasy (Meier 1930; Cane 1936; Munro 1956; Lowenfeld and Brittain 1964; Luca and Allen 1974; Wilson and Wilson 1976)

c. intense desire to make art by filling extra time with art activities (Klar and Winslow 1933; Munro 1956; Kough and DeHaan 1955; Inglehart 1960; Ziegfeld 1961; Hildreth 1966; Luca and Allen 1974)

d. high desire for visual awareness experiences (Munro 1956; Hildreth 1966; Wilson and Wilson 1976)

e. high interest in drawing representationally or to emulate the style of adult artists (Luca and Allen 1974; Wilson and Wilson 1976)

f. self-initiative to make art work (Lindstrom 1957; Peterson 1977)

g. finds satisfaction in engagement in art activities with a high degree of sustained interest (Boas 1927; Kough and DeHaan 1955; Munro 1956; Lark-Horovitz, Lewis, and Luca 1967; Peterson 1977)

h. desire to improve own art work (Lark-Horovitz, Lewis, and Luca 1967)

    i.   persistence, perseverence, enthusiasm, self-motivation to do art work (Fritz 1930; Munro 1956; Conant and Randall 1959; Inglehart 1960; Luca and Allen 1974; Doob 1975; Peterson 1977)

    j.   willingness to explore and use new media, tools, and techniques (Lark-Horovitz 1941; Kough and DeHaan 1955; Munro 1956; Lark-Horovitz, Lewis, and Luca 1967; Luca and Allen 1974; Peterson 1977)

    k.   ambitious for an art career (Hildreth 1966)

    l.   acute power of visualization and a fascination with visual things (Fritz 1930; Munro 1956; Conant and Randall 1959; Wilson and Wilson 1976)

    m.   require a high degree of arousal and motivation (Wilson and Wilson 1976)

    n.   may manifest talents early but talent may not persist into maturity (Fritz 1930; Munro 1976)

    o.   may manifest art talent late, but talent may not persist into maturity (Waddell 1960; Ziegfeld 1961; Hoyle and Wilks 1975; Vernon, Adamson, and Vernon 1977)

    p.   may have motor skills specific to talent; may not have general motor superiority (Manual 1919; Vernon, Adamson, and Vernon 1977)

    q.   easy visual recall from an encyclopedic visual memory; may have a "photographic" mind (Kough and DeHaan 1955; Munro 1956; Conant and Randall 1959; Lark-Horivitz, Lewis, and Luca 1967; Luca and Allen 1974; Wilson and Wilson 1976)

    r.   extraordinary skills of visual perception and a highly developed visual sensibility (Fritz 1930; Meier 1930; Lindstrom 1957; Conant and Randall, 1959; Lowenfeld and Brittain 1964; Luca and Allen 1974; Wilson and Wilson 1976)

    s.   planning of art production activities prior to production (Kough and DeHaan 1955)

3.  Art talent/IQ correlation predispositional behaviors

    a.   above-average IQ is prerequisite to acquire advanced techniques and produce meritorious art (Manual 1919; Hollingworth 1923, 1926; Munro 1956; Inglehart 1960; Ziegfeld 1971; Luca and Allen 1974; Hoyle and Wilks 1975; Vernon, Adamson, and Vernon 1977)

        1.   above-average IQ is necessary condition but not sufficient to guarantee art talent or creativity (Hollingworth 1923; Birch and McWilliams 1955; Schubert 1973; Vernon, Adamson, and Vernon 1977)

2. higher IQ allows development of art talent but does not insure such development (Fritz 1930; Tiebout and Meier 1936; DeHaan and Havighurst 1957; Inglehart 1960; Schubert 1973)

b. representational drawing ability is not dependent upon intelligence (Ayer 1916; Manual 1919; Hollingworth 1923, 1926; Munro 1956)

c. analytic, mechanical, symbolic, and expressionistic drawing are dependent upon intelligence (Hollingworth 1926; Klar and Winslow 1933)

d. intelligence tests do not give indication of artistic talent (Lowenfeld and Brittain 1964)

e. artistically talented students display mature, high-quality behaviors for their age (Fritz 1930; Lark-Horovitz 1941; Lark-Horovitz, Lewis, and Luca 1967)

4. Art talent/subject matter correlation predispositional behaviors

a. do well in science, social studies, and language arts (Yochim 1967)

b. do not do well in mathematics or other curriculum areas that require mathematical skills (Yochim 1967)

c. display as much individuality in their art work as in their handwriting (Hollingworth 1923)

1. superior handwriting is not necessarily correlated with artistic talent (Manual 1919)

B. Observable process behaviors

1. Observable art production process behaviors

a. originality; use of own ideas and idiosyncratic depictions of content (Kough and DeHaan 1955; Ziegfeld 1961; Lowenfeld and Brittain 1964; Gaitskell and Hurwitz 1970; Luca and Allen 1974; Doob 1975; Peterson 1977)

b. demonstration of completion of specific ideas throughout the process of production (Luca and Allen 1974; Peterson 1977)

c. use of subtle and more varied graphic vocabulary than average and will build upon previous visual vocabulary to create new images (Lark-Horovitz 1941; Wilson and Wilson 1976)

d. fluent and experimentive in use of a greater picture vocabulary (Lark-Horovitz 1941; Ziegfeld 1961; Lowenfeld and Brittain 1964; Lark-Horovitz, Lewis, and Luca 1967; Luca and Allen 1974; Doob 1975; Peterson 1977)

e. demonstrates flexibility with ideas when creating art products (Doob 1975)

    f.   displays confidence and comfort with art media and tasks (Peterson 1977)

    g.   demonstrates purposefulness and directness of expression with clarity (Lowenfeld and Brittain 1964)

    h.   demonstrates a clear understanding of structure and sense of the interrelationships of parts in an art work (Lindstrom 1957; Conant and Randall 1959)

2.   Observable art criticism process behaviors

    a.   gives less personal, more objective, reasons for critical judgment of art work of others (Munro 1956; Lark-Horovitz, Lewis, and Luca 1967)

    b.   shows greater, genuine interest in the art work of others and can appreciate, criticize, and learn from the art work of others (Kough and DeHaan 1955; Lark-Horovitz, Lewis, and Luca 1967)

    c.   applies critical insights to own art work (Boas 1927; Lark-Horovitz, Lewis, and Luca 1967)

It is interesting to note the earliest date when certain inquiry about specific topics was reported and whether others have dealt with similar inquiry since that time. There also has been a lack of consistency about kinds of inquiry addressed at various times. For instance, Manual reported that superior handwriting is not necessarily correlated with art talent in 1919 and Hollingsworth claimed that artistically superior students display as much individuality in art work as in their handwriting in 1923. Research about relationships between art making skills and handwriting does not appear to be a contemporary issue. On the other hand, researchers have claimed, from 1919 to 1974, that artistically talented students exhibit highly individualized differences in psychological characteristics and only in the 1970s have Luca and Allen (1974) and Peterson (1977) claimed that artistically superior students demonstrate a completion of specific ideas throughout the process of production. This later claim does not appear to have been an issue to previous researchers.

Some claims appear to be contradictory because researchers have attended to different aspects of a similar problem. For example, several researchers have claimed that artistically superior students will specialize in one subject matter, whereas Kough and DeHaan (1955) claim that these students will draw a wide variety of things. Research about IQ and artistic talent relationships has generated many contradictory claims. Lowenfeld and Brittain (1964) have claimed that results of intelligence tests cannot be used as indicators of artistic talent whereas many other researchers, from

1919 to the present, have claimed that an above average IQ is prerequisite to the production of meritorious art.


## SUMMARY AND CONCLUSIONS

There is an apparent need for research to resolve inconsistencies and contradictions that emerged from past inquiry about artistically talented students. Artistically talented students, as a *unique* research population, have not been studied with the depth of inquiry that exists about students who are intellectually gifted. Therefore, many questions remain unanswered and many problems remain unsolved.

This charcoal study, by a seventh-grade boy, is based upon interpreting a Winslow Homer painting. Artistically talented students often use art works as sources of inspiration and visual ideas. Art work seen in student portfolios will sometimes include such derived images. Photo by Ben Strout.

PART 3  CURRENT TESTING AND
        IDENTIFICATION PRACTICES

*C*URRENT PROBLEMS OF IDENTIFICATION, for any kind of gifted/talented
    program, are frequently examined in relationship to the practice of
testing. Testing, however, is used in a very broad sense to include many forms
of identification procedures. One way to examine current identification practices is to categorize them as the use of (1) standardized tests, (2) informal
instruments, and (3) non-test methods. *Standardized tests* are defined as
ones "in which the procedure, apparatus, and scoring have been fixed so
that precisely the same test can be given at different times and places"
(Cronbach 1969, p. 22). Standardized tests include such instruments as the
Stanford-Binet Intelligence Scale, IOWA Tests of Basic Skills, and the Seashore Measures of Musical Talents. Such tests are also "standardized," as
a procedure, with age/grade norms in order to expand their utility and applicability. *Informal instruments* are instruments that fail to control procedures, apparatus, and scoring so that their results, at different times and
places, are idiosyncratic. Informal instruments include teacher made, class
specific quizzes, performance checklists, and locally developed or single
use instruments of all kinds. *Non-test methods* are procedures, such as self-
nomination, degree of interest or desire, or past academic history, used to
identify and select students for an educational program.

    Although there are many current school, school district, and com-
munity programs designed to serve the specific needs of artistically talented
students, there has been no consensus about recommended identification
procedures or instruments for such programs. No current publication offers standardized, specific guidelines for the identification of artistically
talented students that has been prepared by art educators or other arts professionals. In contrast, many psychologists or educators have written about
academic or intellectual giftedness and have recommended specific instruments and procedures for identification (Guilford 1973; Khatena 1982). Some
recent publications, in response to the six categories of giftedness outlined
in the Marland Report (1972) and used by the United States Office of Education (USOE), have presented various identification practices relative to
each category, including the visual and performing arts. Rubenzer (1979),
in a list of representative tests for the six USOE categories of giftedness,
cites the Horn Art Aptitude Inventory (1953) and the Meier Art Tests (1963)
as visual arts testing instruments. A Center for Global Futures (1981) pub-

lication lists and describes fifty-two currently available standardized tests and twenty-four informal instruments for the identification and selection of gifted and talented students appropriate the USOE categories of giftedness. Three of these formal instruments—the Graves Design Judgment Test (1978), Horn Art Aptitude Inventory (1953), Meier Art Tests (1963—and a locally developed, informal instrument (an Evaluation Form for Art Applicants) are cited as identification instruments for artistically talented students. Khatena (1982) also discusses identification procedures appropriate to each of the USOE categories of giftedness. In a section on identification of visual and performing arts abilities, Khatena cites two standardized creativity tests, three standardized art tests, and two informal instruments. These are the Guilford Creativity Tests for Children (1973), Torrance Tests of Creative Thinking (1974), Horn Art Aptitude Inventory (1953), Knauber Art Ability Test (1935), Meier Art Tests (1963), Advanced Placement Program in Studio Art (Dorn 1976), and Art Talent Behavior Record (Khatena 1982). These sources are clearly reliant upon testing as an identification procedure, although the standardized tests that are recommended have been shown, by others, to have problems and inadequacies for the identification of artistically talented students.

## CREATIVITY TESTS

Guilford and Torrance, authors of major creativity tests, differ in their approaches to measurement. Guilford's (1967) Structure of the Intellect (SOI) model was used to create tasks that measure specific, distinct components of the model, especially as they relate to divergent thinking. Torrance, on the other hand, attempts to measure creativity as results of complex tasks that require simultaneous application of several distinct abilities. Both, however, measure fluency, flexibility, originality, and elaboration as the demonstration of "creativity." Khatena (1982), and others (i.e., Lowenfeld and Brittain 1975) have claimed that visual and performing arts giftedness is closely associated with creativity as a measurable construct. A study in Lincoln, Massachusetts, has shown empirical evidence that raises questions about the use of creativity tests for the identification of artistically talented students. Project Art Band (DeCordova Museum 1982) uses several identification procedures and instruments for selection of visually gifted students. Teacher, other school personnel, parent, and peer nominations are used along with the Torrance Tests of Creative Thinking, Baker's Narrative Drawing Assessment, and Baker's Visual Memory Assessments to identify visually gifted students. In their 1982 report of the Project Art Band, the project staff (DeCordova Museum 1982) reported:

> It might be suggested that the Torrance Tests of Creativity not be included among the instruments used for the identification of visually talented students. It is outdated in that what is scored high for uniqueness has become common place. In addition, many students score high who may be "creative," but are not necessarily visually gifted . . . Project Art Band suggests . . . that the Torrance Tests [of Creativity] not be included among the screening components because of their . . . lack of direct relevance to artistic creativity. (p. 5)

## STANDARDIZED ART TESTS

The Knauber, Graves, Meier, and Horn standardized art tests have been evaluated by a number of reviewers. Many questions have been raised about their possible contribution or applicability to the problem of identification or selection of students for placement in programs for artistically talented students as well as other aspects of art education research.

### The Knauber Art Ability and Art Vocabulary Tests

The Knauber Art Ability Test and the Knauber Art Vocabulary Test (1935) were conceived and published, by the author, to measure art production skills and knowledge of art vocabulary; many questions have been raised, however, about their effectiveness and applicability by Meier, Faulkner, Moore, and Ziegfeld (Buros 1941, 1953) and Eisner (1972). These reviewers have reported that the Knauber tests are not sufficiently complete, measure learned (rather than native) increments and skills, and use many outmoded items that are of little value today.

### The Graves Design Judgment Test

The Graves Design Judgment Test (1948) contains items in which subjects pick the most pleasing, or the best, of several modified images of a single, non-representational design. Application of the principles of unity, dominance, variety, balance, continuity, symmetry, proportion, and rhythm are tested. Claims for a relationship between the results of this test and art production abilities, validity of the construct of aesthetic judgment, clarity of criteria used in this test, ability of results to predict any educational behaviors, and the ease by which subjects might actually mark perceived "right" answers (as opposed to the subject's preferences) have all been questioned by Michael, Ziegfeld, and Shaffer (Buros 1953). The lack of extensive use of this test has also led to questions about its current applicability (Eisner 1972).

## The Horn Art Aptitude Inventory

The Horn Art Aptitude Inventory (1953) is a two-part performance test. In Part 1, subjects are asked to draw twenty familiar objects in a series of timed tasks. In Part 2, subjects are asked to create a series of sketches that incorporate preprinted lines. Palmer and Ziegfeld (Buros 1949, 1953) and Eisner (1972) have questioned the original design of the test as based upon an inadequate sample, that items are too small for subjects to draw upon conveniently, the inconsistent or unclear scoring of items, and adequacy of the test to guide screening decisions for art schools or art awards.

## The Meier Art Judgment and Aesthetic Perception Tests

The Meier Art Judgment Test I and Meier Aesthetic Perception Test II (1963) are designed to measure "aesthetic sensitivity," which is defined as a sense of good organization in a work of art. In Test I, subjects choose the better of two images. In Test II, subjects rank order, from best to poorest, a series of four images. Reviewers have questioned the meaning, completeness, and validity of the aesthetic sensitivity construct, tentativeness of the scoring procedures, incompleteness of the art forms presented, and dated look of the images used. In addition, these tests may measure learned behaviors rather than native abilities, therefore measuring progress in school more than art-related abilities according to Farnsworth, Saunders, Ziegfeld, Schultz, and Siegal (Buros 1941, 1949, 1953, 1972), and Eisner (1972).

The problems raised by reviewers of these few art instruments explain why current writers have often noted an inadequacy of art test development and their lack of use in identification of artistically talented students:

The problem of early identification of those gifted in the visual arts has received sporadic attention over the past several decades. None of the various testing instrument developed during this time has proved useful, nor does the writer know of any serious use of such instruments. (Inglehart 1960, p. 123)

It does not take long to discover that few tests are available in published form in the field of the visual arts. (Eisner 1972, p. 141)

There [are] no completely satisfactory tests of aptitude in art, especially during the school years of individuals. (Khatena 1982, p. 94)

## IDENTIFICATION PROCEDURES CURRENTLY USED

If, despite the recommendations of people outside the visual arts, standardized art tests are not being used, what are the actual practices of identification and selection used in programs for artistically gifted students? We have recently surveyed the selection procedures used in forty-nine programs for artistically talented students offered in schools, school districts, community museums, and state or national programs. These programs are listed in the appendix. *Not one* of these programs uses the standardized tests previously described.

In Table 3, selection procedures used by current programs are reported by category—standardized test(S), informal tests (I), and non-test methods (N)—frequency of use, and percentage of usage in various programs.

Of the nineteen procedures listed on Table 3 most programs use various combinations of procedures although there are few patterns of commonly used combinations. Of the forty-nine programs surveyed, seven programs used only one procedure for identification, seven programs used two procedures, eighteen programs used three procedures, nine programs used four procedures, six programs used five procedures, and two programs used six procedures.

The only procedures used by more than 25 percent of the programs surveyed were self-nomination, a portfolio review, or an interview. Of the possible procedure combinations, the only combination used by more than 25 percent of the programs was the combination of self-nomination and portfolio review. Nineteen programs, 39 percent of the cases, used self-nomination and portfolio review in combination. Of twenty-eight programs that used self-nomination, seventeen (34.7 percent) also used portfolio re-

TABLE 3

## SELECTION PROCEDURES

| Category | Procedure | Frequency | Percentage |
|----------|-----------|-----------|------------|
| | | N = 49 | |
| N | Self nomination | 28 | 57.1 |
| I | Portfolio review | 23 | 46.9 |
| N | Interview | 13 | 26.5 |
| I | Informal art test(s) | 12 | 24.5 |
| N | Classroom teacher nomination | 12 | 24.5 |
| N | Art teacher nomination | 10 | 20.4 |
| S | Creativity test(s) | 8 | 16.3 |
| I | Structured nominations | 7 | 14.3 |
| N | Academic record | 6 | 12.2 |
| N | Parent nomination | 6 | 12.2 |
| S | Achievement test scores | 6 | 12.2 |
| N | Peer nomination | 6 | 12.2 |
| N | Desire/Interest of student | 4 | 8.2 |
| I | Descriptive Checklist | 4 | 8.2 |
| N | Citizenship and Health | 4 | 8.2 |
| N | Art courses taken previously | 2 | 4.1 |
| S | IQ test score | 2 | 4.1 |
| N | Letters of nomination by "others" | 2 | 4.1 |
| N | First come/First serve | 1 | 2.0 |

view; of twenty-three programs that used portfolio review, sixteen (32.7 percent) also used self-nomination. It should also be noted that the majority of programs that used portfolio review are for secondary school identification.

Of the nineteen procedures reported by programs, only three are based upon standardized tests. Of these, the Guilford Creativity Test for Children (1963), Torrance Tests of Creative Thinking (1974), and standardized IQ or achievement tests were named. *None* of the available standardized art tests were used by any of the programs.

Four of the nineteen procedures used were based upon informal instruments. Portfolio reviews, informal art tests, structured teacher nomination forms, and product or behavior checklists were, largely, idiosyncratic. They were generally based upon local criteria generated by local project staffs, although the Renzulli Scales for the Rating Behavioral Char-

When asked to submit a portfolio, artistically talented
students often include a self-portrait. This example, by
a seventh-grade girl, shows advanced understanding of
head proportions, uses pencil lines very effectively, and
is highly expressive. The deliberate use of different types
of lines in the hair, clothing, and shading shows a high
level of sophisticated drawing ability. Photo by Indiana
University AV Services.

acteristics of Superior Students: Artistic Characteristics (Rezulli, Smith, White, Callahan, Hartman n.d.) were specifically named by four program reports.

Twelve of the nineteen procedures used were non-test measures, such as nominations, interviews, and previous school records. Once again, the criteria for evaluation of these measures were largely program specific and idiosyncratic. Nominations of various kinds make up 39.7 percent (N = 62) of the total frequency (N = 156) of the procedures used in all forty-nine programs. Self, classroom teacher, art teacher, peer, parent, and other person nominations simply asked for a personal recommendation. Structured nominations required the person nominating to abide by a set of stated criteria. Desire or interest of students and first-come, first-serve are aspects of self nomination but were stated in program descriptions as separate identification procedures.

## SUMMARY AND CONCLUSIONS

It is possible to consider current testing and identification procedures as reflecting, in a broad sense, the use of (1) standardized tests, (2) informal instruments, and (3) non-test methods. Various writers have recommended procedures in each of these categories. Psychologists and educators, primarily concerned with academic or intellectually gifted students and guided by the USOE categories of giftedness, have compiled annotated lists of standardized tests for each of the USOE categories of giftedness. For the visual and performing arts, a number of standardized art tests have been recommended though their utility for identification of artistically talented students has been questioned by numerous critics. At this time, there are no agreed upon or validated criteria, instruments, or procedures that can be used in visual arts programs in various parts of the country for identification of artistically talented students. As a result, local identification procedures have been developed that are idiosyncratic and particularized to the specific programs in which they are used.

Examination of the most commonly recommended creativity and art tests raises questions about their effectiveness or efficiency as identification procedures for visual arts programs. Art educators have agreed that the currently available standardized art tests fail to serve the needs of identification and selection required for nationally agreed upon criteria.

Actual practices of programs for artistically talented students throughout the country suggest that non-test procedures far outweigh the

use of informal instruments or standardized tests. Self nomination and review of a portfolio, judged by local criteria, are the most frequently used
identification procedures. Most programs for artistically talented students
use a combination of three identification procedures for selection of students. Nominations of various kinds accounted for one-half of the total
number of procedures used in all programs. *None* of the currently available standardized art tests were used in any of the programs surveyed.

The implication of these current testing and identification practices will be set forth in Part 4. Several identification procedures, presently
underutilized, will be reported and recommended and new areas of research
about problems of identification of artistically talented students will be
discussed. Realities of social, political, and economic factors, as they bear
upon identification practices, will be considered as they relate to various
kinds of program organization for artistically talented students.

This is a tempera painting by a fifth-grade boy. Like all children, artistically talented students often depict popular super heroes. In this painting, the dramatic and effective placement of figures and the use of size and cropping display unusual sensitivity. Line, color, shape, and value are all controlled to heighten the drama of the situation. Photo by Indiana University AV Services.

PART 4  RECOMMENDATIONS FOR IDENTIFICATION

$\mathcal{M}$OST EDUCATORS who are interested in identifying talent in the visual arts want to be able, efficiently and effectively, to identify all possible talented students. Many students who are artistically talented are not identified by procedures presently used in the schools. In fact, many school districts do not offer programs for talented art students and, therefore, do not attempt to identify such students. Most students do not take art classes in the later public school years and are not in a school situation where they might be screened as talented. What can be done, at this time, to identify, efficiently and effectively, as many of the nation's artistically talented students as possible?

Schools considering the implementation of a program for artistically talented students need to make decisions about their purposes, program size, and character, before identification decisions are made. In our review of current program procedures for identification of artistically talented students, five to fifteen percent of local school populations were admitted into various programs. Decisions about program size obviously dictate identification procedures to achieve the desired population. Identification procedures should be used that will screen students who will be most appropriate for the types of classes offered. The criteria for entrance into a computer graphics program would differ from entrance requirements for a drawing and painting program. Prerequisite skills, abilities, and experience, therefore, would differ, to some extent, for various kinds of programs. The goals of the program, age group to be served, and types of instruction to be offered, will effect decisions about the kinds of students to be identified.

Several writers (Khatena 1981; Robinson, Roedell, and Jackson 1979; Tuttle and Becker 1980) have suggested that a combination of procedures is the most effective method of identifying gifted and talented students. The battery of procedures used should include diverse sources of information that corroborate the desired characteristics from diverse points of view. As discussed previously, many current visual art programs use a battery of procedures to identify talented students that include standardized tests, informal instruments, and non-text measures.

## STANDARDIZED TESTS

Standardized art and creativity tests were previously described and critiqued. Other standardized tests have been recommended for all types of gifted-talented programs. IQ tests, according to Khatena (1982) and others, are appropriate to use for all five categories of giftedness recognized by the United States Office of Education. Above-average IQ, in most instances, is a prerequisite to successful participation in a program for gifted/talented art students. Achievement test scores are similarly recommended by many current writers (Center for Global Futures 1981; Khatena 1982; Robinson, Roedell, and Jackson 1979; Tuttle and Becker 1980) and the usual criteria is for scores two or more years above grade level.

These current recommendations about using standardized tests were suggested in research reported by Pegnato and Birch in 1959. They focused upon identifying intellectually gifted junior high school students using a battery of screening procedures. These included teacher recommendations, honor role listings, creative ability in art and music, student council membership, superiority in mathematics, and group intelligence and group achievement test results. All students identified by these procedures were subsequently administered the Stanford-Binet Scale to determine their IQ. Effectiveness and efficiency of each of the original battery of procedures were analyzed and reported relative to students with a Stanford-Binet IQ of 136 or higher. Pegnato and Birch found that more than 95 percent of the students identified by all other procedures were identified by combining group intelligence and group achievement tests into one screening procedure. For instance, all students who displayed unusual interest and achievement in music or art were noteworthy in at least two other screening procedures unrelated to music or art. Pegnato and Birch (1959) also found that non-structured teacher recommendations were not effective or efficient as an identification procedure.

## INFORMAL INSTRUMENTS

Several informal instruments were cited previously as currently being used as identification procedures for visual arts programs. These include a portfolio review, local art tests, structured nominations, and behavior or product checklists. Two other informal instruments that are recommended in the gifted and talented literature were not used in the programs surveyed; these are a self-interest and a biographical inventory.

Portfolio Review

A majority of current programs for artistically talented students use portfolio review as an identification procedure and the procedure is recommended by many writers. The advantages of being able to view and critique each student's art work are obvious. Portfolio review does have, however, several drawbacks. Exclusive use of the procedure virtually eliminates identification of potential talent and, as practiced, portfolio reviews are judged by local, idiosyncratic criteria that are often unknown to the applicants. Students with prior art classes and experiences are obviously advantaged in a portfolio review process.

Criteria that are carefully developed, standardized, based upon the judgment of a group of experts, and communicated to applications would be preferable to locally developed criteria based upon subjective judgments. Two models of standardized criteria for portfolio review are currently used at advanced secondary school grades to identify superior students. These are the Advanced Placement Program in studio art and the Arts Recognition and Talent Search program; both programs provide recognition and reward for superior secondary level art students. The selection criteria and processes are provided to applicants and a team of trained judges are used for evaluation of portfolios in both programs. Similar models for various age/grade levels and for a wider audience have yet to be developed. (For an example of an art product evaluation form see Figure 6.)


Local Art Tests

Many local programs administer drawing tasks, or other studio assignments, as an identification procedure. As with portfolio reviews, local and largely idiosyncratic criteria are used to judge the outcomes of such tasks. Criteria are often stated in very open, ill-defined terms such as "creative," "original," "uses color," or "uses form" and these are checked on a prepared form. Such criteria and procedures fail to guide qualitative judgments and are open to purely subjective interpretation. A number of local programs have begun to develop and administer instruments that are carefully conceived and accompanied by criteria systems that can be used to train judges prior to the assessment of art talent (i.e., Lazarus 1981). More needs to be done in the development of instruments that can be used in all parts of the country, accompanied by objective criteria systems, and that include materials for the training of judges.

FIGURE 6

## ART PRODUCT EVALUATION FORM

Name of Student                                              Grade

School                                                      Teacher

Evaluate the student's talent as evidenced in art work on the following scale of 0–5 according to the following criteria. Note that a rating of 5 indicates unique, mature ability and should be used with reservation.

|  | Not evident | Emerging | Average | Competent | Outstanding | Unique |
|---|---|---|---|---|---|---|
| 1. Skillful composition | 0 | 1 | 2 | 3 | 4 | 5 |
| 2. Originality of ideas | 0 | 1 | 2 | 3 | 4 | 5 |
| 3. Complexity and detail | 0 | 1 | 2 | 3 | 4 | 5 |
| 4. Sensitive use of line | 0 | 1 | 2 | 3 | 4 | 5 |
| 5. Sensitive use of color | 0 | 1 | 2 | 3 | 4 | 5 |
| 6. Appropriate use of texture | 0 | 1 | 2 | 3 | 4 | 5 |
| 7. Purposeful use of shape | 0 | 1 | 2 | 3 | 4 | 5 |
| 8. Thoughtful use or space / perspective | 0 | 1 | 2 | 3 | 4 | 5 |
| 9. Effective use of media | 0 | 1 | 2 | 3 | 4 | 5 |
| 10. Expressiveness | 0 | 1 | 2 | 3 | 4 | 5 |
| Column total | — | — | — | — | — | — |
| Weight | 0 | 1 | 2 | 3 | 4 | 5 |
| Weight column total | — | — | — | — | — | — |
| OVERALL TOTAL | | | | | | _____ |

Additional comments: _____

_____

Adapted from: "Evaluation Form for Art Applications," Indianapolis Public Schools, School of Performing Arts. "Instructions for Scoring the Drawing Test, Form E," *Art Enrichment: How to Implement a Museum/School Program.* Austin, Tx: The University of Texas at Austin, 1980. "Creative Products Scale—Art," Detroit Public Schools, 1981.

From *School Arts* (November 1983), used by permission.

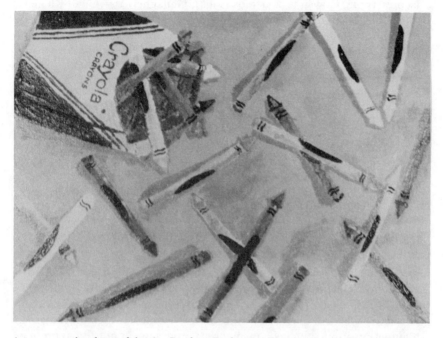

As an example of use of the Art Product Evaluation Form on p. 76, this acrylic paint-ing, by a seventh-grade girl in the Indiana University Summer Arts Institute, would be evaluated as unique in composition and use of space, and outstanding in the other categories. Photo by Indiana University AV Services.

Structured Nominations

Evidence presented by Terman (1925), Pegnato and Birch (1959), Jacobs (1971), Gowan and Demos (1964), Gallagher (1975), and Khatena (1982) demonstrates, over and over again, that an invitation for teachers to nominate "gifted" students has yielded very poor results.

> Teacher ratings . . . tend to overrate the well-disciplined, conforming, mannerly and docile and to underrate the original, creative, curious, and independent. (Gowan and Demos 1964, p. 285)

> Teachers will overlook many gifted children that a well-designed test will find and, conversely, may be overly impressed by the dutiful and hard-working child. (Gallagher 1975, p. 17)

> Teachers do not locate gifted children effectively or efficiently enough to place much reliance on them. . . . A breakdown of those children referred as gifted by the teachers revealed that almost a third . . . were not in the gifted or superior range but in the average intelligence range. (Pegnato and Birch 1959, p. 303)

It is possible to vastly improve teacher nomination effectiveness by providing "structured" nomination forms and in-service education about nomination criteria prior to the nomination process. Some programs for artistically talented students are using these two practices to improve teacher nominations; unfortunately, many other programs do not. Program purposes and goals should guide preparation of structured nomination forms to insure efficient and effective identification of appropriate students who will be suited to, and whose needs will be served by, the school program. (For an example of a structured nomination form see Figure 7.)

Behavior Checklists

Behavior checklists consist of prepared lists of observable behaviors, indicative of gifted abilities in specific categories. Users are asked to check, or rate, the presence of specific behaviors observed for particular individuals under consideration. When rating is added, each behavior is judged for its frequency or strength, as well as its presence.

Most currently available behavior checklists are idiosyncratic, stated in ill-defined or general terms, and often demand too much teacher time in their utilization. A few nationally available behavior checklists for art

FIGURE 7

## VISUALLY/ARTISTICALLY TALENTED STUDENT PROFILE
Nomination Form

| | Seldom | Occasionally | Frequently | Always |
|---|---|---|---|---|
| **Name of Student** | | | | |
| **School**     Grade | | | | |
| 1. Is more apt to respond to artistic peer and adult role models | ___ | ___ | ___ | ___ |
| 2. Possesses a well developed visual memory | ___ | ___ | ___ | ___ |
| 3. Possesses a high curiosity level that stimulates active imagination | ___ | ___ | ___ | ___ |
| 4. Is more apt to respond to environmental observations and changes | ___ | ___ | ___ | ___ |
| 5. Is capable of original thinking | ___ | ___ | ___ | ___ |
| 6. Has the ability to generalize | ___ | ___ | ___ | ___ |
| 7. Examines problems critically | ___ | ___ | ___ | ___ |
| 8. Is able to concentrate for long periods of time | ___ | ___ | ___ | ___ |
| 9. Seeks challenging experiences that are goal-oriented | ___ | ___ | ___ | ___ |
| 10. Engages in compulsive pursuit of special interests | ___ | ___ | ___ | ___ |
| 11. Imposes self-criticism that interferes with satisfaction with task | ___ | ___ | ___ | ___ |
| Column Total | ___ | ___ | ___ | ___ |
| Weight | 1 | 2 | 3 | 4 |
| *Weighted Column Total* | ___ | ___ | ___ | ___ |
| OVERALL TOTAL | ___ | | | |

Additional comments:_____

_____

_____

Adapted from "Characteristics List," *Project Art Band: A Program For Visually Gifted Children.* Lincoln, MA: DeCordova Museum, 1982.

From *School Arts* (November 1983), used by permission.

specific behavior (Renzulli *et al.* n.d.; Khatena 1981) do exist and have been used by programs in various parts of the country. There is still need for greater development of behavior checklists to improve their standardization, clarity of terms, and their ease of utility. Again, the use of behavioral checklists, by parents, teachers, peers, or others requires training that would include clarification of the vocabulary and efficiency of use.

### Self-Interest and Biographical Inventories

A self-interest inventory is recommended by Tuttle and Becker (1980) as an informal instrument that should be filled out by all applicants to a program. Tuttle and Becker specifically recommend a self-interest inventory for visual and performing arts programs that would identify pertinent hobbies and interests that relate to goals of the program. Wilson and Wilson (1981) have developed a prototypic self-interest inventory that has been used informally with other procedures to successfully identify artistically talented students. Their self-interest inventory yields data toward students beliefs about self, general beliefs, goals, and values related to artistic achievement.

The use of biographical information for the identification of artistic talent is recommended by Taylor (1976) and by Ellison, Abe, Fox, Coray, and Taylor (1976) and for all types of gifted-talented programs by Tuttle and Becker (1980) and the Center for Global Futures (1981). Biographical inventories take the form of multiple-choice items, checklists, open-ended questions, or combinations of these procedures. Responses are elicited to questions that concern behaviors and interests appropriate to the goals of the program.

A number of people have noted that many gifted-talented students "display more . . . superior abilities in extracurricular activities than . . . in the classroom" (Tuttle and Becker 1980, p. 55). Biographical and interest inventories can provide insights about individuals that might be overlooked by other school procedures. Wilson and Wilson (1982) report that an intense self motivation to make drawings is the source of "spontaneous art" and that spontaneous art "is usually done at home or in spare and stolen time in school, on the edges of notebooks or on any available paper. . . . Lamentably, this spontaneous art is often ignored and sometimes not seen at all" (p. xv).

The use of a biographical or interest inventory for a visual arts program should seek evidence of self-motivation and non-school art work.

Drawings on spelling papers or arithmetic worksheets should be evaluated as indicators for recommending students to special programs for the artistically talented. Ellison *et al.* (1975) found that biographical information was extremely effective as an identification procedure for artistic talent and that "the biographical approach does not appear to be racially biased as opposed to the more traditional testing instruments" (p. 172). It was, therefore, preferable to standardized test scores or school records for identification of talented students not identified by more typical procedures. (For an example of a biographical inventory see Figure 8).

## NON-TEST MEASURES

A number of non-test measures were cited previously as identification procedures for visual arts programs. These include a variety of sources of nomination, interviews, indicators of student desire and interest, and art and academic school records. One other non-test measure recommended in the gifted and talented literature is structured observation; this procedure was not used in any of the programs previously surveyed.

### Nominations

Unstructured nominations by various persons such as self, peers, teachers, parents, counselors, and others can sometimes provide valuable insights about the individual under consideration. Such nominations, however, depend upon the information and insights provided by the nominator. Bias on the part of a nominator, as well as lack of criteria for nomination, often results in either too little needed or too much inappropriate information. Peer and self nominations are the most valuable nomination of artistically talented students. Students usually know the skills and strengths of other students in the classroom as well as in extra-curricular and other out of school activities. Students are often very self critical and are generally able to assess their own desires and interests and their skills and abilities more perceptively than others. Nevertheless, nomination efficiency requires the preparation of peer and self nomination forms that are appropriate to program goals, relatively clear and easy to use, and easily assessed by program staffs.

FIGURE 8

## BIOGRAPHICAL INVENTORY: *Artistically Talented Students*

NAME _____     DATE _____

Interviews and biographical sketches will yield self descriptions. Indicators of the following characteristics tend to be identified with persons with superior talent.

_____ very responsible and dependable

_____ enjoys reading literary classics

_____ intends to obtain a college degree

_____ adapts to school rules and regulations

_____ has outstanding sensitivity to the environment

_____ perfers traditional and classical music

_____ is highly competitive

_____ is confident and ambitious

_____ stands up for personal beliefs

_____ feels that school lacks adequate facilities

_____ prefers to work alone

_____ admires artistic teachers

_____ recognizes his/her art abilities

_____ prefers an art career

_____ is willing to alter own art work for improvement

_____ spends a lot of time doing art work

_____ uses imagination in day dreaming, story telling, and art work

_____ is aware that others recognize his/her art talent

Rater Comments: _____     _____
                                                                                            DATE

Adapted from: Ellison, R., Abe, C., Fox, D., Coray, K., and Taylor, C. "Using biographical information in identifying artistic talent." In W. Barbe and J. Renzulli, eds. *Psychology and education of the gifted.* New York: Irvington Publishers, Inc., 1975 and Wilson, B. and Wilson, M. Instruments for the identification of artistic giftedness. Paper presented at the NAEA convention, Chicago, Il., 1981.

From *School Arts* (November 1983), used by permission.

### Interviews

A number of programs conduct an interview as an identification procedure following preliminary screening. Sometimes an interview is conducted when portfolios are submitted in person by the applicant. Interviews give the applicant and the interviewer chances to interact and share information in a non-structured, open-ended exchange. An interview should be used to impart information about the program under consideration as well as to collect information about the applicant that might not be available through other sources. Interviews, however, are costly and time consuming and should be used as a final screening procedure.

### Indicators of Desire and Interest

Student desire and interest is probably the most salient identification indicator for identification of artistically talented students. If a program is just beginning or does not have other resources to screen applicants, an indication of desire and interest to participate will yield a fair number of students who might be classified as talented in the arts. Accepting students on a first-come, first-serve basis may seem questionable for a gifted/talented program, however, it will attract highly motivated students and make it possible to enroll students with potential but little previous art experience. Inglehart (1960) has claimed that a persistent interest in the visual arts and a persistence of expressive effort are critical characteristics for identification of artistically talented students.

### Art and/or Academic School Records

Though programs sometimes examine previous art and/or academic school records, such records can be misleading as often as they are helpful (Tuttle and Becker 1980). Some writers claim that high grades are an effective criteria for selection of students for gifted/talented programs; others have pointed out that grades, however, reflect teacher judgments and are an unreliable source. Students who consistently earn high grades are often conforming high achievers, but not necessarily gifted in one or more of the United States Office of Education categories. Conversely, a pool of students, selected on the basis of superior art and/or academic records, will often include a large percentage of those students who would be identified as gifted/talented by other measures.

## Observation

Trained observers can be very accurate in identifying artistically talented students by observing students working in classrooms. It is important, sometimes, to observe students while they are in the process of creating art work as well as to examine their finished products. Observing students behaviors, in general, yields a rich fund of information that would not be available from any other source. For example, the student who constantly draws and doodles on his or her notebook and exam papers is indicating a burning desire to create images. Inglehart (1960), Tuttle and Becker (1980), Wilson and Wilson (1981), and Khatena (1982) all recommend observation as an important aspect of identification procedures. Observation has two major limitations; it is costly and requires trained, perceptive observers who are not regular participants in the student's environment.


## SUMMARY AND CONCLUSIONS

Like many others, we recommend that a battery of diverse sources of information be used as procedures for identifying artistically talented students. The sources used should include standardized tests, informal instruments, *and* non-test measures. Program funding, size, character, and purposes will determine the specific information sources to be selected and used. Yet there are many limitations on objective identification of artistically talented students. There are no agreed upon criteria based upon research findings that are reliable or valid for generalized use. Many questions remain to be answered about salient observable characteristics of art products and observable behaviors of students. Answers to these questions will guide future design of appropriate standardized tests, informal instruments, and non-test measures as efficient and effective procedures for the identification of artistically talented students. Procedures currently used and others that are recommended for use need to be critically examined and evaluated in light of research findings and successful implementation in the field. Much of the required research is yet to be done.

We have previously raised many questions about ambiguities and unresolved questions in the area of identifying artistic talent. We reported specific claims about characteristics of art products and observable behaviors of students with superior abilities in the visual arts and we critiqued standardized tests, informal instruments, and non-test measures currently in use. In these reports, descriptions, and critiques there were many questions raised about the efficacy of current practices.

Past claims about artistically talented students and their art work were outlined and this outline provides a basis for future research. Observable characteristics of art products in respect to compositional arrangement, use of elements and principles, subject matter, and art making skills and techniques need to be researched as a basis for establishing sound and appropriate criteria for the examination and assessment of art products as an identification procedure. Observable, generalized, art-specific predispositional behaviors and process behaviors in art production, art criticism, and art history need to be researched as a basis for establishing sound and appropriate criteria for identification.

The National Assessment of Educational Progress in art (NAEP, 1977, 1981a, 1981b) has created a research based model relative to the work sample technique. NAEP has reported standardized test items and results appropriate to perceiving and responding to aspects of art, valuing art, producing art, knowing about art, and making and justifying judgments about the aesthetic merit of works of art that have been used with nine-, thirteen-, or seventeen-year-old students. The purposes of NAEP are to assess the current effectiveness of instruction in the United States, including art. The norm-based model that has been created can be examined and adapted to the design of instruments for the identification of artistically talented students because it yields distributive data and thus identifies tasks and criteria for several levels and aspects of art ability (see Table 4). The Naive-Sophisticated Model (Clark and Zimmerman 1978a, 1981) presented in Chapter 4, Part 3, sets forth a conceptual framework with sequences of generalized concepts that can also be used to define tasks and criteria needed for the development of instruments to measure many aspects and levels of art capacity and achievement.

The NAEP and the Naive to Sophisticated model include knowledge and ability in art criticism and art history that need to be added to the more commonly used assessment of art products. Relationships between art making, art criticism, and art history skills, knowledge, and abilities are not well understood and have not been researched to any great extent. Art criticism and art history skills have not been used as an identification criteria by most programs. Past overemphasis on art production skills has failed to accommodate other art abilities that might be related to artistic talent.

Identification of artistic talent presents many problems but these are surmountable. There is much research and development that is being done, yet, there is much left to do.

TABLE 4

## NATIONAL ASSESSMENT OF EDUCATIONAL PROGRESS
### *Outline of Art Objectives*

I.  PERCEIVE AND RESPOND TO ASPECTS OF ART

Aspects of art are defined as: sensory qualities of color, line, shape and texture; compositional elements such as structure, space, design, balance, movement, placement, closure, contrast and pattern; expressive qualities such as mood, feeling and emotion; subject matter, including (1) objects, themes (the general subject of a work, i.e., landscape or battle scene), events and ideas (general presymbolic meanings) and (2) symbols and allegories: and expressive content, which is a unique fusion of the foregoing aspects

A.  Recognize and describe the subject-matter elements of works of art

B.  Go beyond the recognition of subject matter to the perception and description of formal qualities and expressive content (the combined effect of the subject matter and the specific visual form that characterizes a particular work of art)

II.  VALUE ART AS AN IMPORTANT REALM OF HUMAN EXPERIENCE

A.  Be affectively oriented toward art

B.  Participate in activities related to art

C.  Express reasonable sophisticated conceptions about position attitudes toward art and artists

D.  Demonstrate an open-mindedness toward different forms and styles of art

E.  Demonstrate an open-mindedness toward artistic experimentation

III.  PRODUCE WORKS OF ART

A.  Produce original and imaginative works of art

B.  Express visual ideas fluently

C.  Produce works of art with a particular composition, subject matter, expressive character or expressive content

D.  Produce works of art that contain various visual conceptions

E.  Demonstrate knowledge and application of media, tools, techniques and forming processes

TABLE 4 *(continued)*

IV.  KNOW ABOUT ART

A.  Recognize major figures and works in the history of art and understand
their significance. (Significance as it is used here refers to such things as
works of art that began new styles, markedly influenced subsequent works,
changed the direction of art, contained visual and technical discoveries,
expressed particularly well the spirit of their age and those considered
to be the major works of major artists)

B.  Recognize the styles of art, understand the concept of style and analyze
works of art on the basis of style

C.  Know the history of art activity and understand the relation of one style
or period to other styles and periods

D.  Distinguish between factors of a work of art that relate principally to the
personal style of the artist and factors that relate to the stylistic period
or the entire age

E.  Know and recognize the relationships that existed between art and the
other disciplines of the humanities (literature, music, and particularly the
history of ideas and philosophy) during a given period

V.  MAKE AND JUSTIFY JUDGMENTS ABOUT THE AESTHETIC MERIT
AND QUALITY OF WORKS OF ART

Statements of aesthetic quality are those that characterize the various aspects of
a work of art, while statements of aesthetic merit are assertions about the degree
of goodness or badness of the work. Justifications of aesthetic merit are based on
criteria such as the degree to which to work is integrated and whether contact with
the work results in a vivid and fused experience

A.  Make and justify judgments about aesthetic merit

B.  Make and justify judgments about aesthetic quality

C.  Apply specific criteria in judging works of art

D.  Know and understand criteria for making aesthetic judgments

Source:  National Assessment of Educational Progress. *Procedural handbook: 1978–1979 art assessment.*
Denver, CO: Education Commission of the States, 1981, pp. 3–4.

This oil-crayon drawing, by a fourth grader, was done in response to a teacher's assignment to depict feelings about living in the city. The single figure, dominated by tall, angular buildings, and a tumultuous sky, express loneliness and fear. The expressive qualities of this drawing are unique for such a young child. Photo by Indiana University AV Services.

## 3
### *Teacher Characteristics and Teaching Strategies*

PART I  REVIEW OF RESEARCH AND INQUIRY
ABOUT TEACHER CHARACTERISTICS

*O*NE OF THE MOST IMPORTANT FACTORS in the education of a student
is an effective teacher, but research tells us little about characteristics of
teachers for gifted/talented students. There has been much speculation
about traits associated with teachers of gifted/talented students that has
lead to unwieldy lists of ideal teacher characteristics. Gold (1965), in response to the number and character of teacher traits that have been generated about education of gifted students, has pointed out that an ideal teacher
for gifted/talented students must be, simply, a "paragon of paragons" (p.
254). Gallagher (1975), Gold (1965), Gowan and Demos (1964), and others
have made it clear that most claims about ideal teacher characteristics have
resulted from armchair speculation. Few studies have contributed defini-
tive lists of characteristics that can be used operationally in program planning by schools or by teacher training programs. Although there is little
research about teachers of the academically gifted, there is a total lack of
a body of research about teachers for students with superior abilities in
the arts.

There is also an unresolved problem in the research that has been
done about teacher characteristics for the education of gifted/talented students. Spaulding (1965), Gold (1965), Khatena (1982), Torrance (1962), and
others have researched teacher characteristics and have established that talented and creative students need teachers with different characteristics and
that use different social and educational techniques than teachers of aca-

demically gifted students but the required differences have not been defined. Research about ideal teacher characteristics for artistically superior students is missing altogether except as it can be inferred or drawn from existing research about education of gifted/talented students.

A quick review of available lists of desired teacher characteristics for teachers of gifted and talented students simply describes desirable traits of teachers of all students. How can teachers of the gifted be differentiated from good teachers in any situation? The differences, like the characteristics of artistically superior students, may be differences in degree, not kind. That is, very little writing about teachers for the gifted and talented has identified any characteristics that are unique only to teachers of gifted and talented students. This claim has been made by Gold (1965), Gallagher (1975), and Gowan and Demos (1964) and many other researchers who agree that listing attributes of ideal teachers for gifted and talented students is an almost impossible task due to lack of research at this time.

The following characteristics for teachers of gifted/talented academic students has been derived from review of many sources. Few of the sources are based upon research and they are simply speculative. Many characteristics are claimed by numbers of sources, implying agreement among those who have thought about the problem of identifying "ideal" teachers for gifted/talented students. We have grouped the claims into two major categories: (1) teacher personality, attributes, and skills and (2) teacher's point-of-view and strategies. Each claim, within each category, is referenced to its source by the names of persons who reported each claim and the date reported.

Teacher personality, attributes, and skills

Considerate, fair, and understanding

(Goodrich and Knapp 1952; Davis 1954; Passow 1955; Committee . . . 1956; Abraham 1958; Strang 1958; James 1960; Crow 1963; Hildreth 1966; Gallagher 1975)

Engages in a wide range of hobbies and activities

(Brandwein 1955; James 1960; Sumption and Luecking 1960; Crow 1963; Hildreth 1966; Bishop 1968; Gallagher 1975; Maker 1976)

Exceptionally well versed in subject matter

(Brandwein 1955; Strang 1958; French 1959; James 1960; Ziegfeld 1961; Crow 1963; Drews 1964; Bishop 1968; Gallagher 1975)

Creative and flexible

(Passow 1955; Abraham 1958; Conant 1958; Sumption and Luecking 1960; Crow 1963; Drews 1964; Hildreth 1966)

Intellectually superior

(Passow 1955; Committee . . . 1956; Conant 1958; Conant and Randall 1959; Waddell 1960; Ward 1961; Gold 1965; Maker 1976)

Possesses large fund of general knowledge

(Henry 1920; Committee . . . 1956; Conant 1958; James 1960; Gowan and Demos 1964; Hildreth 1966)

Enthusiastic and vigorous

(Henry 1920; Carroll 1940; Brandwein 1955; Conant 1958; Ziegfeld 1961; Crow 1963; Gowan and Demos 1964)

Emotionally stable

(Brandwein 1955; Conant 1958; Sumption and Luecking 1960; Crow 1963; Hildreth 1966)

Possesses sense of humor

(Brandwein 1955; Abraham 1958; Strang 1958; Gowan and Demos 1964)

Outgoing and pleasant

(Henry 1920; Abraham 1958; Conant 1958; Hildreth 1966)

Decisive and well organized

(Abraham 1958; French 1959; Brandwein 1960; Gowan and Demos 1964)

The following teacher characteristics were also cited in the literature: good health (Brandwein 1955), fine human being (Goodrich and Knapp 1952), good disposition (Witty 1950), reliable and cooperative (Crow 1963), modest, intuitive, friendly, imaginative, constructive, thoughtful, positive, shows common sense and good will (Abraham 1958).

Teacher point of view and strategies

Possesses favorable attitude toward gifted/talented students

(Carroll 1940; Goodrich and Knapp 1952; Committee . . . 1956; Ziegfeld 1961; Gowan and Demos 1964; Friedenberg 1965; Bishop 1968; Maker 1976)

In this studio scene, a teacher from the Interlochen Center for the Arts has provided a challenging problem and appropriate media and tools for the instructional activity. The student is using techniques and methods of an adult sculptor. Photo by Brill.

Willing to let students proceed on their own

(Passow 1955; Strang 1958; French 1959; Sumption and Luecking 1960; Drews 1964)

Directs each student to maximum achievement

(Goodrich and Knapp 1952; Passow 1955; Conant 1958; French 1959)

Possesses demonstrated teaching abilities

(Carroll 1940; Conant 1958; Barbe and Frierson 1965; Hildreth 1966)

Willing to accept the widest possible sets of solutions to problems

(Passow 1955; Sumption and Luecking 1960; Gowan and Demos 1964)

Makes courses interesting and stimulating

(French 1959; Gowan and Demos 1964; Bishop 1968)

Enjoys teaching

(Davis 1954; Strang 1958; Maker 1976)

Is firm in classroom organization

(Strang 1958; Gowan and Demos 1964; Bishop 1968)

The following teacher characteristics were also cited in the literature: stands up to frustration (Goodrich and Knapp 1952), is skilled in interpersonal relations (Drews 1964), emphasizes student participation (Bishop 1968), emphasizes process oriented teaching (Barbe and Frierson 1965), skilled in developing desirable attitudes (Hildreth 1966), interested in problem solving (Committee . . . 1956), uses student-centered teaching methods (Bishop 1968), is willing to attend in-service classes and receptive to assistance (Barbe and Frierson 1965), and is less patient and more demanding (Gowan and Demos 1964).

## SUMMARY AND CONCLUSIONS

It is interesting to note that characteristics such as sex, marital status, educational background, association with professional organizations, age, and length of teaching experience are not significant factors for differentiating or selecting teachers for gifted and talented students from the general population of teachers (McNary 1967; Bishop 1968). Obviously, teacher personality, attributes, skills, point of view, and strategies for successful teaching of gifted and talented students are more important factors in the selection of teachers for a gifted/talented program. Teachers, with appropriate backgrounds, who are interested in teaching gifted and talented students can be taught the skills and strategies that will improve their future degree of success with these students.

It is also evident in examining these lists of characteristics that most of the writing about desired characteristics of teachers of gifted and talented students was written between 1955 and 1965. Tannenbaum (1979) has described this period of time as a "peak period" (p. 5) of interest in gifted and talented children. Only three publications were cited, prior to 1955, and only six were cited after 1965. Tannenbaum characterizes these periods of time as "deep valleys of neglect" (p. 5). The current interest in education of gifted and talented students is approaching another peak period, but it has not spawned substantial inquiry about desired teacher characteristics.

It is also very obvious that despite the number of characteristics listed above, and frequently reinforced by various writers, few are derived from research or verified by research. The question of ideal teacher characteristics for gifted students remains unresolved. The question of ideal teacher characteristics for students with superior abilities in the arts is virtually unexplored and unanswered at this time.

Personal and individualized attention and direction are important teaching strategies for any successful program for artistically talented students. This Indiana University Summer Arts Institute teacher is helping a student improve her work by directive dialogue and suggestions. Photo by Ben Strout.

PART 2 ORIENTATIONS AND TEACHING PRACTICES

*I*N CHAPTER 1, PART 3, school program planning was viewed as representing three different orientations. Teaching also has been viewed, traditionally, as representing these same three orientations; society-centered, child-centered, and subject-matter-centered. As previously reported, many educational theorists, have discussed how teaching differs as a result of its focus upon society, the child, or subject matter. Contemporary expressions of these traditional orientations, as art education constructs, are found in publications by many art educators. In a democratic society, all three orientations to teaching must be given attention in art education programs that endeavor to improve society, help each person achieve personal fulfillment, and transmit the cultural heritage (Chapman 1978).

## ORIENTATIONS TO THE TEACHING OF ART

In society-centered teaching, emphasis is upon meeting a community's social needs through learning social values and content derived from broad, social problems; learning activities evolve as outcomes of group needs and social interests. The major role of the teacher is as coordinator and mediator of learning, guiding students in their efforts to meet a community's social needs. In art programs, emphasis would be upon helping students understand the role of art in society and the expression of social values through the arts.

In child-centered teaching, expressed interests and needs of students determine the content and structure of the art program; individual problem solving and self-expression are the dominant teaching emphases. The major role of the teacher is as facilitator of student's need for expression and as mentor of the student's need for instruction. In an art program, emphasis would be on helping each student express his or her personal needs and develop his or her capacities and abilities in art.

In subject-matter-centered teaching, emphasis is based upon classified and organized disciplines of knowledge; learning activities emphasize methods, techniques, and findings within separate subject disciplines. The major role of a teacher is as selector of content and instructor of knowledge, understandings, and skills. In an art program, emphasis would be upon perceptual-conceptual inquiry that would develop student capacities for skillful art production, criticism, and appreciation.

The majority of writings about teaching students with superior abilities in the visual arts coincided with a national concern for child-centered teaching and curricula. Goals of increased self-awareness, self-expression, creativity, freedom of choice for the student, and emotional release and stability were freely stated along with protection from imposed adult standards. This era emerged in the 1930s and peaked as a national movement in the 1960s. Art educators' statements reflected this national concern in education:

> The individuality of the child is sacred. (Klar and Winslow 1933, p. 23)
>
> We cannot make a sharp division between enjoyment and use of art . . . we have put enjoyment ahead of use. . . . (Todd and Gale 1933, p. 3)
>
> School has nothing to do with the education or training of artists. It is beyond its possibilities. But what school can and should do is to encourage and not to suffocate the innate creative capacity of children. That is within the scope of the school. (Viola 1942, p. 35)
>
> Value of the art program lies in the enjoyment which each child receives from communicating how he feels and thinks about his own experiences. (Laycock 1957, p. 148–49)
>
> Every child is potentially gifted and 'not gifted' would be absurd for the very foundation of our philosophy is the development of all potential creative ability in every child. (Lowenfeld and Brittain 1964, p. 393)
>
> The art program [at a school for intellectually gifted students] is considered important to the emotional and cultural growth of all the children. Whether or not a child has talent, he can still derive satisfaction from the art experience. . . . Art for the young child is considered merely a means of expression. (Fine 1964, p. 251)

Art educators who held these views imposed restrictions against most forms of directive teaching, even those that were commonly used in the past training of artists. Teachers were told not to allow any form of copying, not to teach techniques, not to criticize, not to display "adult" art work, not to impose adult guidance, and myriads of other restrictions intended to preserve the admired expressiveness of children's work. One form of this movement was the creation of interest groups or clubs in which children were encouraged to express themselves freely—art without instruction. "The Michelangelo Ceiling Society: A Club" (Ashley 1973), with its emphasis upon child-centered art activities, parodies the serious study of art.

In the 1970s, more emphasis upon subject-matter and society-centered instruction and curriculum became apparent. Art educators began to question the restrictive injunctions of the past and to advocate content and purposes derived from sources other than the interests of the child. New teacher's roles for teaching talented students were described:

> It is unwise to offer the gifted a curriculum that is oriented primarily toward media. . . . A conceptual approach to art activities begins with an idea and then asks the child to use materials merely as a means to solving a problem. . . . The gifted child . . . can be guided away from *object-making* into *visual thinking*. (Gaitskell and Hurwitz 1970, pp. 365–66)

> Art is to be stressed as part of the environment . . . to develop a sense of self and community involvement. (Luca and Allen 1974, p. 3)

New emphases upon subject-matter and society-centered goals have led to specified content suggestions and directive activities, yet retained a concern for maintaining each child's individuality and recognition of each child's need for artistic expression. These emphases have not yet become as commonly held or practiced as have many beliefs and practices that represent the child-centered orientation. Some art educators such as Eisner (1969), Efland (1970), Clark and Zimmerman (1978a), and Chapman (1978) have advocated curricula that reflect more current concerns for content-based curricula and that recognize differentiated abilities in the arts.

## APPROACHES TO TEACHING ARTISTICALLY TALENTED STUDENTS

In their book *Models of Teaching,* Joyce and Weil (1972) describe sixteen educational models grouped into four families. Three families are similar to the child-centered, subject-matter-centered, and society-centered orientation previously described. Joyce and Weil claim that the power of an educational model is that it can be applied to the making of curriculum plans, the guidance of teachers' interactions with students, and to specify needs for instructional materials. These three educational activities interrelate as strategies of teaching, although most people think of student/teacher interaction as describing the art of teaching.

We have used these three components of strategies for teaching, suggested by Joyce and Weil, to organize past suggestions for the teaching of students with superior abilities in the visual arts. The following review of suggestions and directives to teachers will be categorized in three headings: (1) directives for curriculum planning, (2) guidelines for teacher-student interactions, and (3) specifications for media and instructional materials. Each claim will be referenced to its source by the names of persons who reported it and the date reported.

### Directives for Curriculum Planning

1. Provide a variety of media for creative expression (Todd and Gale 1933; Hildreth 1952; Greene 1953; Schiefele 1953; DeHaan and Kough 1956, Brittain 1961; DeHaan and Havighurst 1961; Martinson 1968; Tempest 1974)

2. Individualize instruction (Fritz 1930; Erdt 1954; Brittain 1961; Salome 1974; Fox 1979)

3. Present sequences of complex, challenging problems (Boaz 1927; Conant and Randall 1959; Luca and Allen 1974; Salome 1974)

4. Provide enrichment outside the classroom (Erdt 1954; DeHaan and Kough 1956; Luca and Allen 1974; Salome 1974)

5. Create special work for the talented such as posters, cartoons, book jackets, games and puzzles for others, charts and illustrations . . . (Klar and Winslow 1933; Whittenberg 1954; Luca and Allen 1974)

6. Make art activities problem-solving-centered rather than media-centered (Waddell 1960; Gaitskell and Hurwitz 1970)

The following directives for curriculum planning were also reported: provide extra time and special materials and procedures for the talented (Salome 1974), develop each stage to its fullest but do not push realism or thwart growth to protect childishness (Munro 1956), create units of study around emulation of great artists (Gaitskell and Hurwitz 1970), study art of other cultures (Luca and Allen 1974), stress art as part of the environment (Luca and Allen 1974), and stress the elements of design (Luca and Allen 1974).

## Guidelines for Teacher/Student Interactions

1. Don't critique student work, unless child asks, because this hampers creativity (Hildreth 1952; Schiefele 1953; DeHaan and Kough 1956; Laycock 1957)

2. Give guidance, suggestions, or help only as needed (Fritz 1930; Luca and Allen 1974; Tempest 1974; Fox 1979)

3. Use directive teaching, critique, and demonstration to instruct (Domonkos 1978; Jardine 1968; Fox 1979)

4. Answer technique questions only as need arises (Hildreth 1951; DeHaan and Kough 1957)

5. Create self-expression opportunities for all students and outstanding students will emerge (Brittain 1961; Ashley 1973)

6. Emphasize self-expression rather than technique (Fritz 1930; Lowenfeld and Brittain 1964)

7. Do not stress competitive art activities (Fritz 1930; DeHaan and Kough 1957)

Other guidelines for teacher/student interactions include: do not force new materials on the gifted (Lowenfeld and Brittain 1964), use peer tutoring by talented for the average (Salome 1974), do not compare work of the talented with that of the average (Laycock 1957), and discuss each child's abilities with his or her parents (DeHaan and Kough 1956).

## Specifications for Media and Instructional Materials

1. Provide a wide variety of challenging media (Hildreth 1952; Schiefele 1953; DeHaan and Havighurst 1961; Lowenfeld and Brittain 1964; Martinson 1968; Tempest 1974; Gaitskell and Hurwitz 1978)

2. Do not use coloring books, cut-outs, or patterns (DeHaan and Kough 1956; Laycock 1957; Greene 1963; Lowenfeld and Brittain 1964)

3. Use books and films for instructional purposes (Erdt 1964; Martinson 1968)

4. Develop a visuals file about elements and technique and a card file of sequential art activities (Salome 1974)

## SUMMARY AND CONCLUSIONS

Teaching and educating have been defined many different ways by many different professionals. The sources cited obviously disagree about what educational activities should be used as strategies for teaching artistically talented students. For example, some writers stress using media for self-expression in art whereas others stress problem-centered activities rather than media. Critiquing student art work, according to some writers, should not be done unless students request it, while other writers suggest using directive teaching and critiques for teaching artistically talented students.

It should be pointed out that few of the references cited, with recommendations for teacher actions, are based upon research. Just as ideal teacher characteristics in the literature are largely based upon "armchair speculation" (Gowan and Demos 1964), so these lists of suggested curricula, teacher/student interactions, and media and materials are largely without validated research foundations. Obviously, common sense and educational experience are reflected in contents of the lists. Common sense alone, however, should not be used to guide educational beliefs and practices. Educational experience needs to go hand-in-hand with research to build sound educational practice.

Renzulli (1977) has asked, for a long time, that designers of educational programs for gifted/talented students examine how their programs differ from good education for all students. His argument is that good education for all students is, obviously, an important goal. Good education for gifted/talented students, however, must reflect the unique capabilities and capacities these children possess. In just the same way, we must ask, what are the unique characteristics of teachers that would qualify them as teachers of artistically talented students? How should programs, and teaching, for artistically talented students differ from good education for all students? Unfortunately, short of more armchair speculation, answers to these questions remain to be found. Research is vitally needed in both education for intellectually and academically gifted students and for artistically talented students. The paucity of verified research findings about ideal teachers and about appropriate teaching for gifted/talented students cannot be explained, given the long history of concern reflected in the literature cited in this and the preceding chapters.

An enthusiastic discussion is shown between a group of
Indiana University Summer Arts Institute students at the
Fine Arts Museum, Indiana University. The qualities of
a large painting are being observed carefully and will
serve as a basis for a painting assignment to be done, later, in the students' art classroom. Photo by Bob Mosier.

PART 3  RECOMMENDATIONS FOR TEACHING

> It is not uncommon for the uninformed person to say,
> "*Anyone* can teach." Similarly, many professional educa-
> tors believe that *any* teacher can teach gifted children. The
> second opinion is as fallacious as the first. (Gold 1979,
> p. 272)

*I*DENTIFICATION, SELECTION, AND RETENTION of teachers for an educational program for artistically talented students should be guided
by the philosophy and goals of the program. Some degree of match must
be sought so that teachers' knowledge, attitudes, skills, and teaching practices are aligned with the philosophy and goals of their programs. Although
many lists have been generated that purport to describe an ideal teacher
for gifted/talented students, these are not operationally useful. Few of the
characteristics in such lists specify distinct differences appropriate to the
unique needs of gifted/talented students and programs.

## SELECTING TEACHERS FOR
## ARTISTICALLY TALENTED STUDENTS

"The generalization to be developed here . . . is that the teacher
of the gifted [and talented] must possess in abundance those characteristics which can be particularly contributive to the learning to be done by
the gifted [and talented]" (Newland 1976, p. 147). In 1971, the results of
a survey of more than two hundred experts on the education of gifted/
talented students was published in which criteria for selection of teachers
were rank ordered for gifted and artistically talented students and programs
(Advocate Survey 1971). The selection criteria were ranked as follows for
teachers of talented students:

1. Competence in specified skill (art, music)
2. Proven teaching ability
3. Able to relate to children
4. Understanding of special problems in teaching the gifted and
   talented

5. Enthusiasm toward teaching and children
6. Flexibility, open-mindedness
7. Ego strength, self-confidence, maturity
8. Creativity
9. Love of learning, intellectual curiosity
10. Other
11. Strong academic background
12. High intelligence
13. Wide interests

In contrast, "competence in specified skill" was ranked #12 for teachers of gifted students and "proven teaching ability" was ranked #1. "High intelligence," #12 on the teachers of talented ratings, was ranked #7 for teachers of gifted students, above "love of learning," "strong academic background," "creativity," "wide interests," "competence in specified skill," and "other." Interpretation of this data leads to the conclusion that criteria of selection for teachers of gifted students and teachers of artistically talented students may need to differ in respect to some selected characteristics.

Gallagher (1975), however, has observed that "there is probably more nonsense and less evidence dispensed about the needed characteristics of the teacher of the gifted than almost any other single issue" (p. 312). Gold (1979) analyzed several teacher characteristics studies and concluded that they did not differentiate between desirable characteristics for *all* teachers and characteristics of special importance for teachers of gifted/talented students. Furthermore, Gold pointed out that these studies "are more than a decade old and nothing similar to them has been conducted in the intervening years" (1979, p. 279).

Nevertheless, school and community educational programs for artistically talented students are proliferating across the country and their need for teachers and staff members is immediate. Rather than add to past armchair speculations about desirable teacher characteristics, it seems advisable to address teacher's values and attitudes and teacher's behaviors and practices as critical factors in selection and retention of teachers for artistically talented students.

## TEACHER'S VALUES AND ATTITUDES

Teachers who work with gifted/talented students need to examine their beliefs, values, attitudes, and knowledge about gifted/talented stu-

This tempera painting by a fifth grade boy is his interpretation of an image seen on television, the May Day Parade in Moscow. The painting was done as a social studies project as part of a unit about the USSR. Photo by Indiana University AV Services.

dents. Like many persons in the general public, there are teachers who do not understand, resent, or are not sympathetic to the needs of gifted/talented students. Mead (1954) and Tannenbaum (1962) both expressed the opinion that initial reactions of both teachers and students to gifted/talented students are likely to be negative. Weiner and O'Shea (1973) have shown that attitudes of supervisors were more favorable toward gifted students than those of administrators, university faculty members, and classroom teachers, in that order.

On the other hand, Mills and Berry (1979) have found that teachers and parents *of* gifted/talented students hold more favorable attitudes than do regular classroom teachers, administrators, community leaders, or the general public. Experience with, and increased knowledge about, gifted/talented students improves teacher attitudes towards these students. Regular classroom teachers who do not have experience with gifted/talented students, according to Lutz and Lutz (1980), often feel that such children should simply adjust to the usual school schedule or that such children are often outspoken and critical. These conclusions reflect negative biases that many classroom teachers hold.

Torrance (1975), Kaplan (1974), Clark (1979), Tuttle and Becker (1980) and several other writers offer brief activities or exercises that help teachers become aware of their own values and attitudes toward gifted/talented students. None of these activities address attitudes toward artistically talented students but they can be adapted to that purpose. Teachers of aristically talented students need to develop supportive values and attitudes by discussing major issues and beliefs appropriate to goals of the program in which they will teach. One method of assessing teachers' understandings about educating artistically talented students is to have them react to statements and to discuss their reactions as a workshop activity. Such statements as the following might be used to generate discussion and examination of teacher's values and attitudes:

> Teachers can encourage artistically able children simply by having a good supply of basic materials on hand: crayons, paper, paints, clay. Scrap materials, too, will stimulate children to experiment with various kinds of artistic expression. (DeHaan and Havighurst 1961, p. 201)

> Intelligence seems necessary but not sufficient for creativity. Intelligence . . . sets upper limits on possible creativity but *does not* develop creativity . . . especially in above average intelligence ranges. (Schubert 1973, p. 47)

The art program is considered important to the emotional and cultural growth of all the children. Whether or not a child has talent, he can still derive satisfaction from the art experience provided in the program. . . . Art for the young child is considered merely a means of expression. (Fine 1964, p. 251)

The degree of skill present in each gifted child . . . varies from individual to individual. The gifted child's potential may or may not include advanced development of sensory processing or highly developed motor control. (Luca and Allen 1974, p. 14)

As teachers ponder, react to, and discuss these types of statements they will be forced to examine their own beliefs, values, attitudes, and knowledge relative to the education of artistically talented students. Directed workshops, in which program leaders guide the discussion, can be used to screen prospective teachers or train program staffs.

Torrance (1965) has suggested that teachers increase their self-awareness relative to gifted children by indicating characteristics which they would prefer, or not prefer, students to exhibit in the classroom. By adapting the list of characteristics of artistically talented students previously generated (Chapter 2, Part 2), a similar checklist (see Table 5) can be created for in-service workshops for teachers.

Torrance's Self-Awareness Checklist (1965) contains sixty-two separate characteristics and a similar instrument appropriate to raising the self-awareness of teachers of artistically talented students should also present a similarly lengthy list. Some characteristics should be neutral, such as *general motor ability;* some should be very positive, such as *acute powers of visualization.* Some highly controversial characteristics should be listed, such as *highly critical of other's art work,* in order to stimulate discussion and resolution of values and attitudes that are compatible with program goals.

An interesting training instrument, developed by Rader (1975), asks in-service participants to review simulated admission forms for a fictitious national gifted program. Ethnographic, physical, family background, and test data are provided as well as personal data about skills, abilities, goals, and handicaps. Users are asked to recommend or reject each applicant. *After* these decisions are made, the workshop director reveals that the fictitious applicants are based upon real data for such persons as Eleanor Roosevelt, Bill Bradley, Thomas Edison, Barbara Jordan, etc.. Use of this instrument challenges teachers to examine their decisions and to become aware of the great diversity of backgrounds and characteristics of gifted and talented individuals.

TABLE 5

SAMPLE SELF-AWARENESS CHECKLIST

Check the characteristics on the following list that you would like students to exhibit in your classroom. Draw a line through characteristics that you would *not* like students to exhibit.

_____ superior manual skills

_____ good muscular control

_____ independence of ideas

_____ adherence to rules and regulations

_____ freedom from frustration

_____ highly individualistic

_____ superior energy level

_____ haughty and self satisfied

_____ desire to work alone

_____ require high degree of motivation

_____ flexibility with visual ideas

_____ interest in the art work of others

_____ compulsiveness to complete activities

Use of such simulation materials points up the need for teachers of artistically talented students to understand the early development and motivation of art talent. Wilson (1976) has reported the writings of Julian Green, George Grosz, C. S. Lewis, and other artists as they discussed the effects of illustrated books and magazines on their early interests and adult achievement. Wilson believes that "case studies of individual's early art experience is initially the most effective method for developing and adequate theory of motivations which might then be evaluated through the observation of children as they play at their art" (Wilson 1976, p. 59).

A fictional account of the development of an artist may serve the same purpose of building greater teacher awareness and sensitivity for young, artistically talented students. *My Name is Asher Lev*, by Chaim Potok (1972), is a popular book that was on the *New York Times* Best Seller List for six months. Asher Lev, the book's hero, is an extraordinarily talented artist who, ultimately, rejects his family and his faith in the struggle to reach maturity as an artist. This compelling book traces Asher Lev's life through his early childhood and school years while he becomes aware of and develops his artistic talent. The book would be of value to all art teachers and parents who are interested in understanding the development of a young person's maturation as an artist. *My Name is Asher Lev* is clearly record of a young person's sacrifices that are motivated by his unquenchable need to create art. The record of his first crayon drawings to his fully mature paintings is a record of dispute and isolation from people who do not understand his overwhelming need to create art. Discussion of this book in workshops will help teachers examine their acceptance of the child who is driven to make art.

All above recommendations are based upon the belief that teachers' attitudes and values, as well as their knowledge, are crucially important to the sources of a program for artistically talented students. In addition, the training of attitudes and values must conform to the philosophy and goals of the educational program. Awareness building exercises, such as the ones described above, should be held as workshops or in-service activities, on a regular basis to insure consistency and maintenance of positive values and attitudes of program staff.


## TEACHING PRACTICES

Just as teacher's values and attitudes must conform to a program's philosophy and goals, so should teacher's practices. Program leaders have a responsibility to clarify and communicate program philosophy and goals. This is crucial to insuring consistency between orientation of the program and the program components of teacher, student, content, and setting. Whether teachers should act as coordinators and mediators, facilitators and mentors, or programmers and instructors depends upon the philosophy and goals of a program's orientation. Teaching strategies toward social interaction, personal growth, and conceptual-perceptual inquiry should relate to appropriate society-centered, child-centered, or subject-matter-centered orientations mentioned previously. In our review of recommendations for teachers of artistically talented students (Chapter 3, Part 2), for instance, the majority of recommendations were to facilitator or mentor practices relative to a child-centered orientation (i.e., provide a variety of media for creative expression). A few recommendations were to programmer and instructor practices relative to a subject-matter orientation (i.e., present sequences of complex, challenging problems) and only one coordinator and mediator practice related to the society-centered orientation (i.e., create special work . . . such as posters . . . for others). Most teaching practices appear to be based upon a child-centered orientation though all three orientations should be presented in the classroom with learning activities as an out growth of appropriate teacher roles and strategies.

Renzulli (1977) stresses the need for teachers of gifted/talented students to take into account student interests and learning styles through three modes of enrichment. According to Renzulli, gifted/talented students are specifically in need of individual instruction and enrichment content. In his Enrichment Triad Model, Renzulli (1977) presents three types of enrichment that correlate with the three types of teacher roles and strategies we have described previously. Type I Enrichment relates to a child-centered orientation in which individualized learning activities are stressed and the teacher's role is as facilitator and mentor. In Type I Enrichment, general exploratory activities bring the student in touch with learning experiences in which he or she may have an interest. The teacher's role is to set up learning resource centers to nurture student interests and to engage people and community resources appropriate to the interests and needs of individual students.

Type II Enrichment relates to a subject-matter centered orientation in which group projects are stressed and the teacher's role is as programmer and mentor. In Type II Enrichment, methods, materials, and instructional techniques deal with development of thinking and feeling processes. Terms commonly associated with these processes include problem-solving, inquiry training, and divergent, reflective, critical, and creative thinking. Through emphasis on processes, rather than content, students learn abilities which they can use in a variety of learning situations. Type III Enrichment relates to a society-centered orientation in which individual and small group instruction stresses the solving of real problems and the teacher's role is as coordinator and mediator of learning activities. In Type III Enrichment, students become, as nearly as possible, investigators of real problems and topics and use professional methods of inquiry appropriate to the problem. The student takes an active part in formulating the problem and the methods by which the problem will be investigated. Type III Enrichment assumes that there are no *correct* methods or solutions to the problem posed, but students should be able to choose an appropriate model of inquiry, persevere in this inquiry, and produce an adult type product that must be presented to an appropriate audience.

Feldhusen and Kolloff (Feldhusen and Kolloff 1978; Kolloff and Feldhusen 1981) have proposed a similar model, the Purdue Three-Stage Model, in which students are led through a hierarchial progression of enrichment activities developed on a foundation of cognitive and affective objectives. The Purdue Three-Stage Model stresses teaching basic skills along with the acquisition of productive thinking, problem solving skills, and independent research and project planning.

The Renzulli (1977) model emphasizes processes of inquiry appropriate to student's interests and leads students to work in the manner of an adult professional in a specific field. The Feldhusen and Kolloff model (Feldhusen and Kolloff 1978; Kolloff and Feldhusen 1981) emphasizes the teaching of basic skills and content along with similar learning of processes as suggested by Renzulli. Basic skills and content are introduced in increasing levels of sophisitication as students progress through the Purdue Three-Stage Model. Neither of these models specifically address the needs of art teachers or artistically talented students, rather they are addressed to the needs of academically gifted students.

Using these models in a program for artistically talented students, teachers should be aware of program philosophy and goals, plan sequences of meaningful learning activities that incorporate the learning of basic skills and techniques, and the acquisition of processes that would eventually lead to using professional methods of inquiry and production appropriate to the roles of the adult artist, art historian, art critic, and aesthetician.

Teachers of artistically talented students should be aware of students' interests and use resources, such as books, slides, films, art objects, and reproductions to motivate and guide students to produce written accounts about art and to produce studio work. Visits to museums, artists' studios, and visits by local people associated with the arts to the art classroom should be encouraged, whenever possible, as part of a program for talented students in the visual arts. As students are motivated, teaching strategies and teacher roles should always be directed toward imparting basic art skills and art content in increasing levels of sophistication as students progress through the educational program. As student motivation, skills, and learning in art increases, teachers should direct students to assume greater and greater responsibility for generation and execution of art problems in areas of art criticism, art history, and art production. Ideally the

teacher should help students find ways of presenting their individually executed art projects to a public audience for evaluation and criticism; studio
work might be shown in individual and group exhibitions and written inquiry could be published. These exhibitions and publications should be
responded to by local art critics and other members of the community. In
this way, talented art students progress from learning basic skills and content to creating art projects that resemble the work of adult professionals.


## SUMMARY

Ideal teacher characteristics for gifted/talented programs have been
generated by great numbers of writers. Unfortunately, these are unrealistic
because they are either idealistically unattainable or they fail to differentiate between good teachers for *all* students and good teachers for gifted/
talented students. Past research has indicated that programs for intellectually or academically gifted students and for artistically talented students
should differ. Specifically, the need for competency in specified skills are
more crucial for teachers of artistically talented students.

Teachers' values and attitudes are amenable to change and program directors should conduct staff sessions in which major issues are analyzed and discussed, staff members should express and examine their own
beliefs, values, attitudes, and knowledge about artistically talented students.
Such sessions should be used to form values and attitudes to be supportive
of and consistent with the expressed philosophy and goals of a specific program. One method that can be used for increasing awarenesss is to have
teachers read accounts of the development of art talents and abilities in
biographical, autobiographical, or fictional reports.

Teaching practices used in a program should also conform to, and
act in support of, a program's philosophy and goals. Deliberate consistency
and conscious awareness should be sought so that a variety of appropriate
practices will be used by teachers toward the attainment of diverse goals.
One method of incorporating such goals and practices is to consciously
develop cycles of learning experiences based upon an ordered sequence of
planned stages. Each stage should be defined to include appropriate teacher
roles, strategies, and practices along with content and experiences that are
consistent to the stage's goals.

Research is needed to further define characteristics of those persons who would be most effective as teachers of artistically talented students. Methods and materials need to be developed for educating teachers

toward examining their beliefs, attitudes, values, and knowledge about artistically talented students. Most available methods and materials have been developed expressly for teachers of academically or intellectually gifted students; models for teaching and program organization also exist for education of the gifted. Such models, however, do not necessarily address the educational needs of artistically talented students. We have suggested some ways that such models can be adapted for teaching the artistically talented though much more needs to be done. Theoretical research about proper teaching practices for students talented in art and applications to classroom practice are critically needed.

On a field trip to the University greenhouse, a seventh-grade boy from the Indiana University Summer Arts Institute, captured strange cactus shapes in this pen and ink sketch. The bold use of line and texture and the variety of shapes used create an incisive statement about the prickly cacti. Photo by Nancy Shake.

# 4
## *Curriculum Content*

PART I  REVIEW OF RECOMMENDATIONS
FOR CURRICULUM CONTENT

 *A*CCOMMODATION TO INDIVIDUAL DIFFERENCES BETWEEN STU-
DENTS has a long history in American schools. Art teachers and art curriculum designers have proposed many different ways of accommodating
artistically superior students in classrooms. Like other practices in the
schools, various suggestions about art curriculum content have reflected
general social, political, and economic influences on the schools at different periods of time. Feldman (1970) has discussed effects of social and
political pressures on the schools and the need to accomodate to individual differences. He has pointed out that children are capable of understanding differences of ability and interest in artistic creation and that they are
not "bruised" by this awareness. He goes on to say, "one does not gain any
insight into the democratic process by pretending that all youngsters are
capable of equal levels of artistic or other achievement" (p. 53).

### ORIENTATIONS TO CURRICULUM CONTENT

Society-centered, child-centered, and subject matter-centered orientations to the teaching of art were described in Chapter 3, Part 2. These
orientations can also be discussed in relation to curriculum design and implementation. In a society-centered curriculum, the content and learning
experiences would emphasize individual and group activities toward social
goals such as a community improvement mural project. A child-centered

curriculum would emphasize content and learning activities that encourage personal goals such as freely expressing oneself through a variety of art media. In a subject-matter-centered curriculum, the content and learning activities would emphasize knowledge, understanding, and skills about art, such as understanding of one's artistic, cultural heritage. The content and learning activities for all three orientations include selections from art production, art history, art criticism, and aesthetics.

Three orientations to curriculum design (society-centered, child-centered, subject-matter-centered) and four sources for content and learning activities (art production, art history, art criticism, aesthetics) will now be used as organizers to discuss some curriculum activities for artistically talented students that have been suggested in the past. Historically, there do not appear to be art curricula specifically designed for talented art students that specify content and learning activities other than recommendations for enrichment or supplemental activities. Developmentally structured curricula for grades K–12, specifically designed for artistically superior students, are rare if not lacking. Most of the recommendations are stated as generalized objectives for artistically superior students rather than as structured curricula or content models that specify art content drawn from sources such as art production, art history, art criticism, or aesthetics.

It should be noted that the following outline is based primarily upon idiosyncratic, supplemental activity recommendations from the past. Specific recommendations will be outlined and each recommendation will be referenced to its origins by the source and date reported.


## Society-centered curriculum recommendations for artistically talented students

### Art production

1. Make posters or serve as poster chairperson for local drives and holidays (Meredith and Landin 1957; Brittain 1961)

2. Aid less talented students in completing art projects (Meredith and Landin 1957; Hopkins and Shapiro 1969)

3. Create art projects that stress social studies projects and group cooperation (Ashley 1973)

4. Assemble materials for group projects for class use (Whittenberg 1954; Hopkins and Shapiro, 1969)

5. Hold community exchange art exhibits (DeHaan and Kough 1956)

6. Make games, puzzles, and scrapbooks for children in the hospital (Whittenberg 1954)

## Art History

1. Learn about art and daily living (Gold 1965)

## Art Criticism (none)

## Aesthetics (none)

## Child-centered curriculum recommendations for artistically talented students

### Art production

1. Make vocabulary charts, illustrations, class portraits, posters, cartoons, puppets, newspaper covers, etc. (Klar 1933; Whittenberg 1954; Hopkins and Shapiro 1969; Treffinger and Gowan 1971; Ashley 1973; Luca and Allen 1974)

2. Use art for self-expression to aid psychological development (Osburn and Rohan 1931; Cane 1951; Hildreth 1952; Brittain 1961)

3. Stress media experimentation (Brittain 1961; Erdt 1962; Hildreth 1962)

4. Provide a table with scraps or odds and ends for free expression and creation of new forms of design (DeHaan and Havighurst 1961; Williams 1970; Tempest 1974)

5. Paint a mural, build a diorama, make period dolls, and other group projects (DeHaan and Kough 1956; Ashley 1973; Luca and Allen 1974)

6. Make individual projects such as an art diary, drawings from music, make abstractions, and toothpick sculptures, etc. (DeHaan and Kough, 1956; Ashley 1973)

### Art history (none)

### Art criticism

1. Keep a file of great pictures and discuss moods and how the pictures make you feel (DeHaan and Kough, 1956).

### Aesthetics (none)

This photograph, by a boy in an Advanced Placement Class at New Trier Township High School, was done for a Numbers and Letters assignment. The assignment stressed photography skills as well as use of numbers and letters as imagery. Photo by Larry Kirsch.

Subject-matter-centered curriculum recommendations for artistically talented students

## Art production

1.  Learn and use technical knowledge and vocabulary (Hubbard 1967; Rice 1970)

2.  Develop perception skills to form, color, design, and space (Gold, 1965; Hubbard 1967)

3.  Emulate achievements of artists in order to improve skills and master media (Hubbard 1967; Gaitskell and Hurwitz 1970)

4.  Develop skills and techniques in drawing, painting, and clay work (Luca and Allen 1974; Peterson 1977)

5.  Emphasize free-hand drawing of museum objects (Klar 1933)

## Art history

1.  Develop appreciation for artistic heritage through reading, viewing films, visiting art galleries and museums, etc. (Laycock 1957; Erdt 1962; Hildreth 1962; Hubbard 1967; Martinson 1968; Rice 1970)

2.  Learn art history vocabulary and symbols (Hubbard 1967; Rice 1970)

3.  Relate art work to other periods of time (Luca and Allen 1974)

## Art criticism

1.  Study art reproductions to learn art appreciation (Laycock 1957)

2.  Study works of art to develop artistic taste (Gold 1965)

## Aesthetics

1.  Train the individual sense of aesthetics (Osburn and Rohan 1931)

2.  Sensitize organization of knowledge to aesthetics as background for art production (Freehill 1961)

3.  Learn philosophical definitions of aesthetic forms (Rice 1970)

## SUMMARY AND CONCLUSIONS

Obviously, the majority of past recommendations have been directed toward art production activities. Art history, art criticism, and especially aesthetics have not received as much attention or definition. Yet these are important aspects of complete curriculum content for artistically talented students because they are suited to complex, in-depth study and help students understand the entire spectrum of the study of the visual arts.

The question raised by Renzulli (1977) as to how educational programs for gifted/talented students differ from good education for all students is not answered by most of these curriculum recommendations. On the other hand, Brittain (1961) has said that "a good art program for the talented is also a good art program for those who . . . are not considered artistically talented" (p. 298). This argument is not resolved. Eisner (1966) and others call for programs that provide opportunities for artistically talented students to study art in depth and that a substantial portion of their school day should be set aside for that purpose.

It appears that what is really needed, in terms of curriculum content for talented students, are content structures that accommodate the needs of all students. We will describe one such structure (in Chapter 4, Part 3) as an example of a content structure that accounts for the needs of the most naive to most sophisticated visual arts students. This structure defines a wholistic visual arts education, with content devised from professional roles in the visual arts, in a developmental sequence that meets the needs of all students who study the visual arts.

This student, at the Interlochen Center for the Arts, is centering clay on a potter's wheel just as a professional ceramicist would do. Programs for artistically talented students often provide experiences in which students learn art skills and techniques used by professional artists. Photo by Brill.

PART 2  CONTENTS AND STRUCTURES OF
CONTEMPORARY PROGRAMS

*T*HERE ARE MANY PROGRAMS IN THE UNITED STATES for artistically
talented students offered at elementary, junior high, and senior high
school levels. Organization of those programs includes in-school, out-of-
school, school, museum, magnet and specialized schools, and summer settings. The types of program emphases are numerous and varied. Contents
generally stress many types of art production and, to a much lesser degree,
art history and art criticism. Teachers for these programs for artistically
talented students include local art teachers, museum docents, professional
artists, college and university faculty, graduate students, and undergradu-
ate pre-service students. We have gathered information from about sixty
current programs for artistically talented students that require criteria for
entrance. The following discussion is based upon forty programs that have
provided detailed information about their levels, settings, emphases, content, and faculty.

## LEVELS AND SETTINGS

The programs we reviewed are sometimes offered at several different grade levels. For example, a summer program may serve students from
grades one through twelve or a museum program may serve students at the
junior and senior high levels. The forty programs reviewed offer different
organizational groupings. For example, one large city program may report
an elementary component, a junior high component, and a senior high magnet school.

Included within the forty programs reviewed, there are sixty-one
components: nineteen elementary schools, seventeen junior high schools,
and twenty-five secondary schools. *In-school programs* (N = 8) offer special art classes during all or part of the school day; *summer programs*
(N = 10) offer special art classes in the summer, and *magnet and specialized schools* (N = 15) offer artistically talented students special art classes
at one site and attract students from the entire school district or offer resi-
dential arrangements, at one site, for students throughout the country, are
the three most popular types of program organization. *Out-of-school pro-*

*grams* (N = 4) include after school clubs, evening classes, and Saturday classes, and *school/museum programs* (N = 3) in which museum facilities and personnel are an integral part of the program, are also offered as types of education for artistically talented students. In-school programs are offered about equally at elementary and junior high levels and less frequently at the senior high level. Summer programs are offered more frequently for senior high school students than for students at grades one through eight. Magnet and specialized school programs are significantly more common at the senior high school level; extra school programs are significantly more common for students in grades one through six. Magnet school and school/museum programs are typically offered in large cities where there are large numbers of students and museums that can support educational programs. Summer programs are frequently offered at college and university campuses; they may be supported by state and local boards of education or by the college or university that will organize the program and supply the facilities.


## PROGRAM EMPHASES

Programs at different levels and settings often report their program goals but, only occasionally, offer a philosophy statement. The program emphases are so diverse and dissimilar that commonalities are difficult to find. Emphases range from generalized critical thinking development to skills and techniques for preparation of professional artists.

Most programs emphasize some form of enrichment based upon art experiences with specific media. At the secondary level, many programs emphasize acceleration through development of art skills in specific media. Along with media experiences, many programs claim other processes and emphasize other goals. A number of programs stress critical thinking skills, also referred to as visual thinking or problem solving. Self expression, child expression, and individualized art experiences are terms found often in descriptions of program goals. The learning of elements and principles of design are still found, commonly, in goal statements. Unified, interdisciplinary, and comprehensive understanding of the arts are frequently mentioned as goals, especially at the elementary level. Several high school programs emphasize preparing students for careers in art. Many programs, at all levels, use artists in the classroom to demonstrate art making skills and to serve as a role model for artistically talented students. A number of art programs are offered, at the elementary level, as an enrichment program for intellectually or academically gifted students, although most of the programs reviewed in this chapter are designed specifically for artistically talented students.

## CONTENT

There is a decided art production emphasis in contemporary programs for students talented in the visual arts (Table 6). There are about thirty different art production activities specified as curriculum content in the sixty-one program components reported. The most popular, commonly offered art activities are, at all levels, drawing (49 percent), painting (46 percent), ceramics (36 percent), sculpture (34 percent), photography (31 percent), and printmaking (30 percent). These are also art activities offered most frequently in regular art classes. As is also true of regular art classes, exploratory art production activities predominate in elementary schools and become less frequent in secondary schools. Conversely, specific media activities are more frequently offered in secondary schools. Drawing is offered in thirty program components and, of these, 76 percent are offered in secondary schools and only 16 percent are offered in elementary schools. Of the nineteen programs offering photography, none are reported in elementary school programs, 35 percent are offered in junior high programs and 52 percent are offered in high school programs. Twelve art production activities are only offered at the secondary level. In senior high schools, many programs purport to prepare artistically talented students for specific arts careers. Art activities related to this emphasis and reported only at the high school level are design, commercial art, animation, tv/video, fashion art, drafting, theatre design, interior design, and portfolio preparation.

A number of art production activities are reported in 5 percent or less of the program components. These activities include fashion art, color theory, tv/video, illustration, animation, puppetry, drafting, creative sound, stained glass, illustration, theater and interior design, and bookbinding. Many art activities were mentioned only once in the program components reported. This may be due to the availability of art teachers and/or professional artists with specific media skills. Few programs offer a rationale for the inclusion or exclusion of specific art activities as curriculum content.

Art history is offered as a specified art activity in 31 percent of the total program components reported. It is only offered in 26 percent of the elementary programs, 35 percent of the junior high programs, and 32 percent of the senior high programs. Art criticism is offered as a specific ac-

TABLE 6

## PER CENT OF PROGRAM CONTENT REPORTED IN 61 CONTEMPORARY PROGRAM COMPONENTS FOR ARTISTICALLY TALENTED STUDENTS

| Activity | All Components N = 61 | Elem. N = 19 | Jr. Hi. N = 17 | Secondary N = 25 |
|---|---|---|---|---|
| Drawing | 49% | 16% | 47% | 76% |
| Painting | 46% | 21% | 53% | 64% |
| Ceramics | 36% | 21% | 35% | 48% |
| Sculpture | 34% | 16% | 35% | 48% |
| Art history | 31% | 26% | 35% | 32% |
| Photography | 31% | * | 35% | 52% |
| Fibers/Fabrics | 31% | 21% | 18% | 48% |
| Printmaking | 30% | 5% | 29% | 48% |
| Art criticism/appreciation | 18% | 16% | 18% | 20% |
| 2D Design | 13% | * | * | 32% |
| Portfolio preparation | 13% | * | * | 32% |
| Graphics | 11% | 11% | 12% | 12% |
| Jewelry | 11% | 11% | * | 16% |
| Architecture | 10% | 11% | 12% | 8% |
| 3D Design | 10% | * | 6% | 20% |
| Computer graphics | 8% | 5% | 18% | 4% |
| Metals | 8% | * | 6% | 16% |
| Commercial art | 8% | * | * | 20% |
| Calligraphy | 7% | 5% | 12% | 4% |
| Film making | 7% | 5% | 6% | 8% |
| Foundations | 7% | 5% | 6% | 8% |
| Fashion art | 5% | * | * | 12% |
| Color theory | 5% | * | * | 12% |
| TV/Video | 5% | * | * | 12% |
| Illustration | 5% | 5% | 6% | 4% |
| Animation | 3% | * | * | 8% |
| Puppetry | 3% | 5% | 6% | * |
| Drafting, Creative sound, Stained glass, Theater design, Interior design, Book binding | 2% | * | * | 4% |

* not offered

tivity in 16 percent of the elementary, 18 percent of junior high programs, and 20 percent of the senior high programs. It is possible that art history and art criticism are also offered as integral parts of other art classes and not as separate classes though this was not reported by most programs.


## TEACHERS

A majority of the forty programs reported for artistically talented students are based in public schools; the largest category of teachers in these programs (50 percent), therefore, are local certified art teachers. These teachers also are found in extra-school, museum, and summer programs. Professsional artists (27 percent) and museum docents (5 percent) are found as teachers in in-school, out-of-school, magnet, museum, and summer programs for artistically talented students. College and university faculty (9 percent), graduate students (9 percent) and art methods preservice students (14 percent) usually teach in summer programs but may also be found in other types of programs.


## SUMMARY AND CONCLUSIONS

There are many more programs offered for artistically talented students than is commonly believed. Several school districts or individual schools reported that they believed they were the "only" schools offering a program at their level and in their type of educational setting. There are many similarities, as well as differences among the program content and organization found in these programs for artistically talented students. There is great need for an information sharing network among schools and other agencies that are offering elementary, junior high school, and senior high school programs for artistically talented students.

There are more programs offered at the senior high school level than at elementary or junior high school levels. In-school, magnet and special school, and summer programs are the most popular organizational structures. Art activities became more specialized, and diverse, in these programs as students increase in age and expertise. A career emphasis becomes most obvious at the secondary school level.

Few programs make apparent their philosophy or long range goals. As a result, rationales and justifications for program content and activities

As a result of studying about Van Gogh and his art work and style, an eighth grade boy painted this water color interpretation of a Van Gogh painting. Such activities should help talented students generalize what they learned and what they use in their own art work. Photo by Ben Strout.

are often lacking. It appears that programs are based upon available facilities and faculty more frequently than on a curriculum structure that contains a philosophy specific to the education of artistically talented students. Most programs attempt to offer a curriculum with enrichment and acceleration experiences, but the experiences do not differ greatly from the regular school art program.

The major contribution of these programs is to bring together artistically talented students and support their study of art to develop art related knowledge, understanding, and skills that would not be possible in regular school settings. Students also become aware, through participation in such programs, that there are other talented students like themselves and they receive a chance to interact with each other, sharing their common needs and interests. In addition, such programs bring these students into contact with faculty with specialized art skills, professional artists, and other professionals in the arts, thus providing role models and career possibilities for students whose skills and interests are in the arts.

Traditional fine arts subjects such as drawing, painting, sculpture, ceramics, and printmaking are the most frequently offered art classes. Other art classes such as photography, graphics, architecture, and fibers are examples of other art experiences offered in addition to more traditional art classes. Emphasis upon more traditional fine arts offerings is important in developing students' knowledge, understanding, and skills about the visual arts that provide a basis for study of other, less traditional, art experiences. When art production is the sole emphasis of a program for artistically talented students, however, important knowledge, understanding, and skills related to the study of art history, art criticism, and aesthetics are denied. That fewer than one-third of the programs reviewed offer art history classes or cite art history as a program emphasis, and that less than one-fifth offer art criticism, indicates less attention to these vital components of understanding the arts than is given to the thirty art production activities listed.

Despite these criticisms, there are many more programs offered for artistically talented students than there were a decade ago. Most programs report their inception within the past five to eight years. Despite minimal funding, support, and facilities, in many cases, programs for artistically talented students are beginning to become more numerous and are gaining greater recognition than in the past. Once established on firm foundations, these programs need to develop curricula that will be based upon individual needs and abilities of artistically talented students and that are consistent with a sound philosophy and well-constructed goals appropriate to such students.

This pen and ink drawing, by a college freshman, shows a vast knowledge and understanding of the work of Dürer, a 16th Century artist. In this sophisticated drawing, the student has created a novel self-portrait done in the style of a great master. Mastery of the use of line, shapes, perspective, value contrast, and detail, as well as symbols come together in a unified and impressive composition. Photo by Indiana University AV Services.

PART 3  A CURRICULUM MODEL FOR LEARNING
EXPERIENCES IN THE VISUAL ARTS

*C*URRICULA FOR INTELLECTUALLY GIFTED STUDENTS often stress advanced conceptions and sophisticated ideas. Students who are gifted in science, mathematics, social studies, and language arts are often offered accelerated or enrichment programs that are adaptations from regular school curricula. Learning in the visual arts, for students who are artistically talented, also requires curricula that stress advanced understanding, knowledge, and skills about the visual arts. Curricula in the visual arts, however, are not usually structured as they are in other subject matters. To accelerate and enrich knowledge, understanding, and skills in the visual arts is, therefore, more difficult.

In most art classrooms, there is a continuum of demonstrated skills and abilities ranging from those with indifferent or naive talent to those with profoundly sophisticated talent. Availability of an educational structure with content that encompasses teaching naive to sophisticated students would be useful for art teachers who desire to accommodate students, in the same classroom, with various levels of ability. Opportunities for acceleration and enrichment learning activities are predicated upon content structures that accommodate a variety of levels of achievement.

A lack of curriculum structures in the visual arts that accommodate students with various abilities may be explained, in part, by examining some of the most common goals claimed for the field of art education. Art teachers have sought a great number of diverse goals for their students: increased creativity, self-identification and self-fulfillment, perception training, increased social adjustment and mental health, environmental awareness, cultural awareness, social equality, overcoming handicaps and disabilities, and increased understanding of mass and other communication media. None of those diverse goals take as its starting place or end point the unique qualities, experiences, or content of art as a subject matter nor do they emphasize the unique contributions that the qualities, experiences, or content of art may make toward a person's education.

The study of art is essential in an educational program that aims to develop, in all students, those social, personal, and cognitive skills that are necessary for responsible participation in a democratic society. As part of the general curriculum, an appropriate art curriculum should promote students' social, personal, and perceptual/conceptual development through art. As a discipline in its own right, art should be studied to help students understand and appreciate the feelings, ideas, and values that the major traditions of art communicate. Without art as both a separate discipline and as a part of the general curriculum, students' learning experiences are incomplete.

The activities of professionals working in the areas of art history, aesthetics, art criticism, and art production suggest appropriate learning experiences for art students (Clark and Zimmerman 1978a, 1978b, 1981). This idea is not new; science, music, mathematics, and other disciplines have long taught advanced students to understand and emulate the work of adult professionals in these fields. But what do practitioners in art history, aesthetics, art criticism, or art production actually do? What knowledge and skills must they possess? How did they arrive at their present positions? Answers to these questions are essential to the establishment of content and structure for unique art education programs.

Artists are those who create works of art. Art critics interpret and criticize works of art. Art historians place works of art in stylistic and historical contexts. Aestheticians generate theories about art and aesthetics and develop criteria by which to judge works of art.

Artistically talented art students should know and experience each of the four roles, artist, art critic, art historian, and aesthetician, with full acknowledgement of each separate professional role. Visual arts education programs should develop their character specifically from recognition of differences among these roles, clarification of role differences when assumed by the learner, and full recognition of the contribution of each role toward a wholistic art education. From this basic construct, it is possible to identify and define content for learning experiences that are appropriate to each role, while maintaining an awareness that each role is an integral part of the complex and unique subject matter of art.

Art education programs that would educate toward increasing students' sophisticated understanding of adult professional roles in the field would be justified much as science, music, mathematics, and other subject matters have used knowledge about professional roles in justifying their place in educational programs in the schools. Like these other subject matters, the content of a visual arts educational program needs to be ordered in developmental sequences appropriate to the needs of learners. Any structure for learning experiences in the visual arts should rest on the important supposition that learners enter their study of the visual arts in a naive, uninformed state and exit in a sophisticated state as a result of planned teacher interventions and sequenced educational activities. This concept has been presented in Chapter 1, Part 2, where talent is discussed as a normally distributed characteristic.

As a curriculum development and evaluation structure, we have described the continuum of naive to sophisticated levels of learning as divided into seven stages (see Table 7). In this continuum, the learner moves from a hypothetical naive stage (NN) to a still naive stage (NNs) that encompasses some germinal understandings. At this stage, learners require introductory, readiness experiences. These experiences prepare learners for teacher interventions and educational encounters at a rudimentary level, that are intended to decrease the learners' naiveté and contribute minimally to their sophistication. At the next stage (Ns), the learners' decreased naiveté and emerging sophistication provides a background for more difficult learnings. Intermediate and more advanced learner tasks, directed by planned teacher interventions and educational encounters, further decrease naiveté to the point where the learner reaches higher stages (NsSn and Sn) in which sophisticated understandings and skills begin to predominate those that are more naive. Further attainment of understandings and skills moves learners to a stage (SnS) where their sophistication is demonstrated at a near mastery level, though still including some naiveté. The ideal end stage (SS) is defined by achievement of the most highly sophisticated understandings and skills related to professional roles in the field. The entering stage of the naive learner (NN) and the exiting stage of the sophisticated professional (SS) are hypothetical. The naive learner is assumed to be an individual of any age who is just beginning to study the visual arts. The end stage is actually an ideal toward which most professionals continue to work; it recognizes that a person's education is never completed. The ideal end stage is defined by achievement of highly sophisticated understandings and skills related to four professional roles in the discipline of art.


## CONTENT FOR LEARNING EXPERIENCES
## IN THE VISUAL ARTS

Sequences of content that focus upon important skills and understandings relative to each role will now be described for the structure shown in Table 7. Clarity and accuracy in the teaching of art demands carefully conceived programs with discrete learning activities. Four or five content strands, relative to each professional role, will be used to differentiate discrete learning activities. Each content strand, within each role, will be described with introductory to mastery level activities appropriate to a learner's development. Some strands begin only at an intermediate or advanced stage because learners must experience tasks at introductory and rudimentary levels of related strands before entering these more advanced strands.

TABLE 7

## A STRUCTURE FOR LEARNING EXPERIENCES IN THE VISUAL ARTS

| Hypothetical Beginning Stage | Stages of Teacher Interventions and Levels of Educational Activities | | | | | Ideal End Stage |
|---|---|---|---|---|---|---|
| NN<br>Naive Stage:<br>Entering Behaviors | NNs<br>Introductory | Ns<br>Rudimentary | NsSn<br>Intermediate | Sn<br>Advanced | SnS<br>Mastery | SS<br>Sophisticated Stage:<br>Professional Roles |
| 1.<br>Unskilled maker of art. | | | | | | Artist: creator of works of art confirmed by a community of experts. |
| 2.<br>Producer of purely subjective reports and uninformed judgments about a work of art. | | | | | | Art Critic: producer of public statements about works of art that are interpretations and judgments based upon objective criteria. |

| | | | | Art Historian: producer of public statements about historical relations and cultural contexts of works of art that may be confirmed or denied by a community of experts. |
|---|---|---|---|---|
| 3. Producer of reports that demonstrate lack of awareness of works of art in a historical context. | | | | |
| | | | | Aesthetician: producer of public writings about the nature of art, art theory, and artistic standards that may be confirmed or denied by a community of experts. |
| 4. Producer of purely subjective reports and uninformed preference statements about works of art. | | | | |

Sources: Clark and Zimmerman (1978a, 1978b, 1981).

Until learners have experienced most of the tasks at earlier levels, they should not be expected to complete mastery level tasks.

### Artist: Content Strands

1. *Media and Skills* are developed from introductory, manipulatory experiences with media to rudimentary, intermediate, and advanced experiences in which the limitations and possibilities of specific media are explored. These experiences lead to mastery level uses of media and skills in the creation of a work of art.

2. *Concepts and Knowledge* about the making of art begin with introductory, exploratory experiences with art concepts. Tasks that relate increasingly skillful uses of media to applications of concepts and knowledge are required at the rudimentary, intermediate, and advanced levels. At the mastery level, understanding of concepts and knowledge are demonstrated in the creation of works of art.

3. *Critique of Learners' Art Work* begins after learners have had manipulatory experiences with media and exploratory experiences with concepts. Appropriate critique skills are developed at rudimentary, intermediate, and advanced levels. At the mastery level, learners qualitatively critique their own art work in process and after completion.

4. *Personal Style in Learners' Art Work* emerges only at an advanced level of development, derived from previous learning experiences and familiarity with a variety of artists' styles. It culminates in demonstration of a mature personal style at the mastery level.

### Art Critic: Content Strands

1. *Vocabulary and Categories of Description* are developed from introductory experiences in which learners use an undifferentiated vocabulary of description and end with the ability to categorize works of art through accurate description and analysis at the mastery stage.

2. *Phenomenological and Contextual Criticism* begins with simple familiarity with works of art. Directed description and analysis experiences, emphasizing qualities observed within a specific work of art, lead to advanced and mastery level exercises of description, analysis, interpretation, and judgment based upon phenomenological aspects of the work of art. At advanced and mastery levels, environments within which works of art

are created are also studied, leading to the ability to criticize an art work both phenomenologically and contextually.

3. *Methods and Stances of Art Critics* will be understood as a consequence of a sequence of learning experiences that begin with undifferentiated discussion of works of art and are developed through many directed, oral criticisms of specific works of art. At an advanced level, learners read, study, and analyze extant art criticism in order, untimately, to understand the work of art critics at a mastery level.

4. *Criticism of Specific Works of Art* begins with subjective, undifferentiated judgments about works of art. These experiences lead to learning experiences that clarify differences between subjective and objective criteria and judgments and personal interpretations of specific works of art.

5. *Meta-Criticism* is introduced only at an advanced level when various points of view and methods used by critics are studied. At the mastery level, learners generate criticism of the work of art critics.

Art Historian: Content Strands

1. *Socio-cultural Interpretation* starts with general awareness of social and cultural influences on works of art. Then, learners become involved in tasks that develop greater understanding of the influence of society and culture on artists and their works. At a mastery level, learners are able to write socio-cultural interpretations of works of art.

2. *Methods and Techniques of Art Historians* are taught from rudimentary technical descriptions and classifications of works of art to intermediate and advanced placement systems and skills of increased specificity. At the mastery level, learners identify and authenticate individual works of art.

3. *Art History Research* involves, at an introductory level, simple awareness of a time continuum in respect to works of art. Next, learners study various forms of art history inquiry and theory. With this background, learners generate theory about art history, at the mastery level, that is based upon criticism of the writings of art historians.

Aesthetician: Content Strands

1. *Vocabulary and Categories of Description,* at the introductory level, involves untutored discussions of works of art. Learning experiences, from intermediate to advanced levels, involve the use of an increasingly ac-

curate vocabulary of description and categorization skills. These experiences culminate, at the mastery level, in learners' use of refined vocabulary and categorization skills when discussing works of art.

2. *Standards of Quality* at the introductory level takes the form of common sense aesthetic criteria that are used when discussing works of art. As learners progress, they learn to use rudimentary, intermediate, and advanced sources of aesthetic criteria applied to work of art. Learners produce, at the mastery level, statements about standards of quality for works of art based upon established aesthetic criteria.

3. *Preference Through Aesthetic Standards* is developed from rudimentary to advanced exercises in describing, analyzing, and interpreting qualities in works of art based upon aesthetic criteria. The ultimate outcome is experiencing and valuing art works aesthetically, resulting in the attainment of refined taste.

4. *Essays about Aesthetics* are introduced at the intermediate to advanced levels. Learners study the writings of aestheticians to learn about philosophical methods of research. This strand culminates in learners writing essays, based upon aesthetic research, about appreciating and valuing works of art.

5. *Art Theory* is studied only at the advanced level. Diverse and congruent theories about the nature of art are examined. At the mastery level, theories are generated about the nature of art and aesthetics.

## APPLICATION OF THE STRUCTURE TO EDUCATING STUDENTS TALENTED IN THE VISUAL ARTS

This structure, with content strands, explicates educationally sound sequences of generalized concepts. These have utility for curriculum and program design in visual arts education and applicability to the needs of individual students of the visual arts. The structure was used as an outline for the content of *Art/Design: Communicating Visually,* a junior or senior high school text book which we wrote in 1978. This book presents learning experiences, in media units, based upon the stages, roles, and strands outlined in this content structure. Lessons within each unit provide acceleration and enrichment opportunities for students of various levels of achievement.

Acceleration in a visual arts curriculum would mean the attainment of increased precision of meaning and understanding of specific aspects of producing, conceptualizing, and talking and writing about works of art. In an acceleration program, the talented student would move from more naive stages to more sophisticated levels of achievement at a more rapid pace than the average visual arts student. The sequence of horizontal stages (introductory, rudimentary, intermediate, advanced, mastery) for each of the professional roles (artist, art critic, art historian, aesthetician) would provide content for learning experiences that outline a program for accelerated attainment of learning outcomes.

Enrichment in a visual arts curriculum would mean the attainment, at any stage, of increased depth of understanding of contents of each strand within each role and of interrelationships among knowledge and skills related to the four professional roles. In an enrichment program, the talented student would study relationships between art production, art criticism, art history, and aesthetics. Interrelated study of all four professional roles, at more sophisticated stages, would lead to an enriched understanding of the visual arts.

In Table 7, acceleration represents increased horizontal movement across the stages. Enrichment represents vertical, in-depth experiences within a role and between roles at any given stage. Gallagher (1975) has pointed out that "relatively little attention has been paid to the actual content that would make up the heart of any differentiated program [for the gifted]" (p. 32) and has urged the development of more complex curriculum units and materials, for the gifted, that are based upon more advanced conceptualization of a subject. The visual arts content structure described in this chapter establishes a form and defines an outline for relevent content for learning experiences in art. In doing so, it structures the actual content for differentiated programs and more complex curriculum units and materials for students who are gifted and talented in the visual arts.

In the Indiana University Summer Arts Institute, students worked intensively for several hours per day in the medium they chose. An eighth-grade girl, who had never done printmaking, created this skillful linoleum cut after experimenting with printing techniques for only 1½ weeks. Photo by Ben Strout.

*Educational Settings and*
*Administrative Arrangements*

PART I  REVIEW OF
ADMINISTRATIVE ARRANGEMENTS

$\mathcal{S}$CHOOL ADMINISTRATORS AND PARENTS have long supported the need
for differentiated services for children whose IQs are below normal.
Argument for an *equal need* for children who are as different, but whose
IQs or artistic abilities are above the norm, has not been accepted as read-
ily. There has been much accessibility to special school services for students whose IQs are at or below 70, but few similar services are offered
for artistically talented students. The most common argument has been
that children with superior intelligence or talent do not need special school
services; they can "make it on their own." This has been disproved many
times and the Marland Report (1972) specifically defined gifted children,
including those with superior artistic abilities, as those who, by reason of
their superiority require services or activities not ordinarily provided by
the school.

As early as 1928, Goddard claimed: "it is even more desirable to
segregate the gifted than the defectives. We have learned to segregate the
defectives because they cannot do the work that is given to the regular children in the grades. We should segregate the bright children because they
can do more and better work than the regular children" (p. 35). Bentley,
in 1937, contributed to understanding deviation IQ differences: "The gifted,
like the feebleminded by way of analogy, are misfits in the regular classroom . . . like the inferior, the gifted require special attention and provi-

sions that will assure them the right of proper training for individual and social advance" (p. 171).

Thom and Newell discussed the "hazards of the high IQ" in a 1945 article. Their argument is that although children with a 70 or a 130 IQ may appear normal in size and appearance, their reactions to school expectations will differ drastically from those of regular children. The child with a 70 IQ will be frustrated by inability to keep up whereas the child with a 130 IQ will learn quickly and may become bored. Although the symptoms of these children's learning problems differ, the magnitude of the problems are essentially the same. Similar differences, and degrees of differences, exist between naive art students and highly talented, sophisticated students that might well be enrolled in the same classes.

## BACKGROUND: 1850–1920

Accommodation to extreme individual differences of superior students has taken many forms in American schools. Most adaptations began in the late 1800s with a few large city public school systems initiating ability grouping and limited promotion or grade-skipping. By 1900, grade skipping and flexible promotion, such as double or half year promotion, had become popular. Other accommodations for superior students included vacation schools, mentor programs, credit by examination, individualized instruction, and special classes (Heck 1940).

In 1901, the first special public school for academically superior students, in the United States, was opened in Worcester, Massachusetts. The school was attended by superior students from throughout the Worcester school district (McDonald 1915). During 1915 to 1918, Los Angeles, California, initiated and developed an enrichment program for superior students that came to be known as Opportunity A Classes. Such classes were based upon ability grouping at various grades and special enrichment units and activities were developed (Heck 1940). By 1920, special schools and programs of various kinds, for gifted and talented students, were established in large cities such as New York City; Cincinnati, Ohio; Elizabeth, New Jersey; Santa Barbara, California; Detroit, Michigan; and Rochester, New York. University communities such as Urbana, Illinois were also experimenting with special education programs for superior students. In 1921, Cleveland, Ohio, also initiated its Major Work Class enrichment program that continues to operate to the present.

## BACKGROUND: 1920–1950

During the early 1920s, two major developments in American education influenced special programs for superior students, the Progressive Education Movement and the research of Lewis Terman. The progressive Education Movement had become very popular and had effected the character of the country's schools. Proponents of this movement questioned removing children from their age groups for special classes. They advocated heterogeneous, self-contained classes at each grade level and development of enrichment materials to be used with superior students in such classes. As a result, ability grouping and grade skipping almost disappeared during the 1920s and 1930s (Chaffee 1963) except in certain large city school systems, such as Cleveland and New York.

In Chapter 1, Part 1, Terman's research was described. In 1921, Terman inaugurated the long series of investigations that are reported in the *Genetic Studies of Genius*. This research attracted much attention to superior children and established use of the Stanford Binet intelligence test, and specific scores on that test, as a reliable identification instrument for gifted students. Obviously, the Terman studies triggered a continuous stream of scientific study that has continued intermittently to this day. The attention Terman's studies attracted, particularly after publication of the first volume of *The Genetic Studies of Genius* in 1925, renewed school and public concern for gifted children and for some special accommodation to their specific needs in the schools. This concern was expressed, even during the Progressive Education era, in special classes for superior students in a few selected schools throughout the country.

In 1935, Cohen and Coryell called for a Central Arts High School, in New York, to be organized for gathering all the aesthetically gifted children in the city. As an outgrowth of its elementary and junior high school programs for superior students, New York City established specific cluster schools, in 1938, such as the Bronx High School of Science and the High School of Music and Art. Students from throughout the city were offered opportunities to compete for entry into these schools. They were admitted on the basis of their academic performance and their science and mathematical abilities or artistic superiority in music or the visual arts. Soon after, in 1941, Hunter College established the Hunter College Elementary School as a cluster school for gifted students and in 1955 the Hunter School for Girls was designated as a secondary school for gifted girls (Hildreth 1966). These and other designated schools in New York and other cities were established despite the Progressive Education Movement's admonitions against homogeneous ability grouping.

## BACKGROUND: 1950 TO THE PRESENT

The 1950s witnessed a renewal of interest in various forms of accommodation to the needs of public school gifted students. In 1954, however, though one-half of the nation's secondary schools had special low ability grouping, only 4 percent had special high ability arrangements such as grouping (Freehill 1961).

Specific programs for the gifted have been initiated, experimentally, in many parts of the country. The majority of gifted education programs now in existence were initiated during the 1960s and specific programs for artistically talented students are a very recent phenomenon. New developments in gifted education, such as programs focusing upon early childhood, gifted handicapped, culturally different gifted, and rural gifted, began in the 1970s and continue into the 1980s as expressions of new concerns in the education of gifted/talented students. Hurwitz (1983) has written a guide to program planning for students who are gifted and talented in the visual arts in which creating supportive environments is discussed. Madeja (1983) has edited a volume of reports that describe fourteen successful contemporary programs for the gifted and talented in art education. Since 1982, The Gifted/Talented Times, in *School Arts* magazine, has reported programs, products, and publications for teachers of talented visual arts students (Clark and Zimmerman, 1982–). A special 1983 issue of *School Arts*, 8 (2), was devoted to the education of artistically talented students.

## ADMINISTRATIVE ARRANGEMENTS FOR GIFTED/TALENTED STUDENTS

A number of persons who have written about gifted and talented education have discussed the principle methods of administrative arrangements that are used in the public schools. There is great similarity among these discussions and consensus that the major administrative arrangements are enrichment, ability grouping, and acceleration, though these specific terms are not always the ones used in various texts (Kough 1960; Freehill 1961; Gowan and Demos 1964; Rice 1970; Clark 1979; Morgan, Tennant, and Gold 1980; and Khatena 1982).

Table 8, adapted from Kough (1960), summarizes major administrative arrangements used in school programs for gifted/talented students. However, it is important to note that "the kinds of programs for teaching

TABLE 8

## BASIC ADMINISTRATIVE ARRANGEMENTS
## FOR GIFTED CHILD PROGRAMMING

I.   In-class Enrichment

II.  Ability Grouping

    A.   Specialized schools

    B.   Special classes in regular school for all of the school day

        1.   Classes recruited from one school

        2.   Cluster classes recruited from several schools

    C.   Special grouping for only part of the school day

        1.   "Pull-out" classes

        2.   Special courses

        3.   Grouping for non-school activities

    D.   Grouping for out-of-school activities

III. Acceleration

    A.   Grade skipping

    B.   Early admissions

    C.   Rapid progress through an educational sequence

        1.   Accelerated progress programs

        2.   Advanced Placement programs

        3.   Credit by examination

the gifted have usually been summarized under the three terms: ability grouping, acceleration, and enrichment. Such a classification is misleading because it suggests that the three are mutually exclusive. Instead, they are more often interrelated and interwoven" (Hildreth 1966, p. 183).

Enrichment, ability grouping, and acceleration are simply administrative arrangements that permit and facilitate the development of gifted/talented students' unique abilities and that support the development of learning materials for that purpose. These arrangements are also frequently offered simultaneously in various programs. Decisions to adopt any of these arrangements does not preclude the use of the others. "There is no law that says that all three of the possible adaptations . . . cannot be included in a single program" (Gallagher 1975, p. 269).

### In-class Enrichment

Enrichment means providing individualized instruction to gifted/talented students who remain in heterogeneous classes with their age peers. Enrichment occurs when gifted/talented students are challenged to do problem solving, individualized work, and creative and critical thinking that is beyond the interests and abilities of other students in the class. An expansive discussion of enrichment and its use in gifted/talented education is contained in a book by Renzulli (1977), where he describes general exploratory activities, group training activities, and individual and small group investigations of real problems as three types of enrichment.

In the art classroom, enrichment occurs when teachers direct highly talented students into individualized inquiry and in-depth art production, art criticism, art history, and aesthetics experiences based upon their developing skills. In Chapter 4, Part 3, a structure for the design of enrichment experiences in the visual arts is described. Claims such as "the fine arts, well taught, are enrichment classes, *per se*" (McWilliams 1964) or for instrumental art activities in music, science, or social studies to serve as art enrichment activities (Barnes 1963) are false. They are false because (1) they are not based upon recognition and adaptation to individual differences in ability and (2) they are not based upon enriching the basic subject matter of art.

### Ability Grouping

Ability grouping, also known as tracking, clustering, homogeneous grouping, etc., means the bringing together of students with similar abilities for all or parts of their school experiences. Various ability grouping arrangements include special classes within a school, cluster schools within a district, or simply groupings for part of the school day, including extra-school activities such as art clubs. For the purpose of the following discussions, in this and the subsequent chapter, the following definitions of ability groupings will be used.

*Specialized school* are schools designed for gifted/talented students within an administrative unit, such as New York's Music and Art High

School, or with open enrollment for students from any part of the country, such as the Interlochen Arts Academy. *Special classes in regular schools* includes classes in which students are recruited from each school's regular attendance area or "cluster classes" in which one school offers special classes to students from several adjacent school attendance areas. *Special grouping for part of the school day* includes "pull-out" classes in which students are taken from their regular classroom for specialized instructional experiences, special courses in which students are grouped by ability levels and offered adapted content and instruction, such as Honors courses or atypical art content, and grouping for non-school activities in which district administrated activities occur outside the regular school schedule, such as evening classes, Saturday classes, and art clubs. *Grouping for out-of-school activities* includes all specialized offerings that are administered by other organizations than public schools, such as museums, colleges, and universities, including museum classes and summer-school programs.

Dallas' Booker T. Washington High School and similar junior and senior high schools in other cities across the country are examples of cluster or magnet schools within a district. These schools attract talented students within a specific district by offering programs designed to meet their unique educational needs. Such schools, however, exist for a very small percentage of students across the country who exhibit special talents in the arts. Few school districts are able to offer the qualified staff or unique facilities required for specialized or cluster schools. Throughout the country, the most frequent ability grouping in the visual arts takes the form of out-of-school activities. Sponsored art clubs, private lessons, Saturday schools, museum classes, and summer art camps are frequently the only source of opportunities for ability grouping that are offered to students with talent in the visual arts. Ability grouping in the classroom usually means academic subject groupings such as language arts, arithmetic, social studies, and science. Ability groupings in art, music, drama, and dance are usually considered beyond the responsibility of the public school. Students who are talented in the visual arts usually attend "two" schools; their regular classes during the school day and extra art classes after the school day. Recently reported research by Bloom (1982) describes this phenomenon relative to one hundred young, gifted, high achievers. The young artists in this research, like the others, usually studied with a first teacher, a local teacher who was not highly skilled in art. These students then sought a second teacher who used individualized teaching methods and was more highly skilled in art. They then sought a master teacher who was an expert in their field of interest. The second and/or master teachers were sought at great sacrifice because they were rarely available in the local schools or community (Pines 1982).

Acceleration

Acceleration is an administrative arrangement that permits individual students to progress more rapidly than other students through the school program. Practices such as promotion, early admissions, and more rapid progress are various forms of acceleration. Pressey (1949), Keating (1979), and Stanley (1977) all advocate greater use of acceleration and claim that extensive research reviews provide positive evidence for acceleration without any detrimental effects. A structure for the design of acceleration experiences in the visual arts is described in Chapter 4, Part 3. The following definitions of various acceleration practices will be used.

*Grade skipping* is the promotion of students from one grade to a higher grade, out of their regular grade sequence. Grade skipping was more commonly used during the 1940s and 50s and is no longer a popular practice.

*Early admission* to an educational program permits students to enter a program before they meet the standard age/grade admission requirements. The most common examples of early admissions are to kindergarten, first grade, high school, or college.

*Rapid progress through an educational sequence* includes accelerated progress programs that combine several grades into one grade, Advanced Placement courses at the high school level that offer advanced college admissions credit, and credit by examination by which students may receive credit for taking a course simply by earning a high score on an examination.

Acceleration systems exist for subject matters, such as mathematics, in which linear development and grade level sequences of topics are clearly established. Art, as it is taught in the schools, lacks both of these characteristics and, therefore, acceleration is rarely used for artistically talented students. This is true despite such claims a "Acceleration is considered quite advisable in such skill aspects of art subjects as . . . drawing" (Birch and MacWilliams 1955, p. 26).


SUMMARY AND CONCLUSION

Concern with various administrative arrangements for gifted/ talented students has always been countered by fear that identifying and providing special programs for gifted/talented students will create "conceited little prigs" (Goddard 1928) or elite sub-groups. Alexander (1981) believes that "art educators do not want to be identified with an elitist movement which would convey negative connotations for the images of average students in art" (p. 45). Goddard and numerous researchers since his time have shown that these concerns are without foundation. Popularity of the administrative arrangements surveyed in this chapter indicates their considered use in schools all across the country; their effectiveness and practicality are demonstrated daily.

A prevailing opinion of many art teachers, expressed by Luca and Allen (1974), is that "the gifted can remain with their classmates and take additional classes or seminars—departure from the group may have an adverse effect" (p. 26). Studies have shown, however, that enrichment, ability grouping, and acceleration have consistently shown successful results (Worcester 1976). Questions remain about the advantages of one administrative arrangement over another and which arrangement would be most successful given specific educational settings. Art teachers need to explore the advantages, for their artistically talented students, of these arrangements in order to provide the best educational experiences possible. In the next part, successful contemporary programs in art education will be discussed that use various administrative arrangements for educating students with superior abilities in the visual arts; recommendations for future practices will also be presented.

Many contemporary programs for artistically talented students are offered in, or work in conjunction with, local museums. This provides opportunities for students to have experiences that would not be available in regular classrooms. For example, this young student is observing the dramatic composition and swirling figures in a large, imposing painting in the Fine Arts Museum, Indiana University. Photo by Bob Mosier.

PART 2  ADMINISTRATIVE ARRANGEMENTS AND
RECOMMENDATIONS FOR
CONTEMPORARY PROGRAMS

*T*HERE ARE TWO PROBLEMS related to the reporting of contemporary
use of various administrative arrangements for artistically talented
students in contemporary programs. One is lack of agreed-upon definitions of vocabulary describing arrangements and the other is the use of
other terminology, by those who describe programs, than that which is
typically used. Information reported in this chapter, therefore, is based partly
on interpretation of forty program reports. Of the three types of administrative arrangements (enrichment, ability grouping, and acceleration), only
three instances of the use of in-class enrichment are reported. Fifty-seven
instances of ability grouping and sixteen instances of acceleration are reported. It is very possible that enrichment is practiced more frequently than
it is reported, but enrichment has not been featured in the forty program
descriptions and announcements that were reviewed for this chapter.

## PROGRAMS AND ADMINISTRATIVE ARRANGEMENTS

The outline presented in Table 7 in the previous chapter lists administrative arrangements under three basic types. The forty programs reviewed reported an average of approximately two different administrative
arrangements used within a program. Some programs used only one administrative arrangement and many programs used two or three within a
single program. As noted in the previous chapter, simultaneous use of several administrative arrangements is a common practice in contemporary
programs for artistically talented students.

The forty programs reported in this chapter represent many different types of programs. They include two for primary school age, fifteen
for elementary school age, sixteen for junior high school age, and twenty-
three for secondary school age students. Many of these programs attract
students from regions that are not defined by public school district bounda-
ries or attendance areas. Summer classes, school-museum programs, and
magnet schools often attract students from many schools into one program.

There were seventy-six instances of various kinds of administrative arrangements reported for the forty programs reviewed for this chapter. As expected, there are far more out-of-school opportunities (30 percent) for artistically talented students than types of in-school administrative arrangements (see Table 9). Specialized schools, as cluster or magnet schools (18 percent), are the most popular type of school option offered to artistically talented students though these are predominantly offered at the junior and senior high school levels. Accelerated progress, generally as non-graded grouping, is offered in 14 percent of the programs, though predominantly in out-of-school activities. Pull-out classes represent 13 percent of the instances reported, predominantly in elementary school components of programs. Special classes in one school, limited to one school's attendance area (5 percent), special or cluster classes in one school that draw upon adjacent school attendance areas (3 percent) and in-class enrichment (4 percent), are less common administrative arrangements for artistically talented students than for academically or intellectually gifted students. Non-school activities, including art clubs and evening or Saturday classes comprise only 3 percent of the instances of administrative arrangements reported in this review.

Three administrative arrangement possibilities (grade skipping, early admission, and credit by examination) are used in academic or intellectually gifted programs but are not reported by any program for artistically talented students. These arrangements are dependent upon measurable progress and attainment of advanced skills in an accelerated manner. As we have pointed out, art programs typically do not provide these options, in large measure due to the lack of coherent sequences of instruction. Some specialized schools, however, do teach sequenced programs in which accelerated progress or credit-by-examination ought to be possible.

## In-Class Enrichment

Most researchers and educators would agree with Kough (1960) that enrichment should provide students with a variety of learning situations, materials, and activities to give him or her a depth and breadth of learning experiences beyond those offered in regular program. Enrichment does not mean adding more of the same kinds of materials or activities for the gifted and talented that would be available in the regular classroom. There are two types of enrichment cited in the literature. Lateral or horizontal enrichment, according to Havighurst, Stivers, and DeHaan (1955), is non-accelerative enrichment that maintains the students' age-grade levels and encourages them to broaden their interests and be introduced to

TABLE 9

## ADMINISTRATIVE ARRANGEMENTS USED IN CONTEMPORARY VISUAL ART PROGRAMS FOR ARTISTICALLY TALENTED STUDENTS

|  | Frequency in 40 programs | Instances N = 76 |
|---|---|---|
| Out of school activities | 23 | 30% |
| Specialized schools | 14 | 18% |
| Accelerated progress | 11 | 14% |
| Pull-out classes | 10 | 13% |
| Advanced Placement | 5 | 7% |
| Special classes in one school, within one school | 4 | 5% |
| In-class enrichment | 3 | 4% |
| Special classes in one school, from many schools | 2 | 3% |
| Special courses | 2 | 3% |
| Non-school activities | 2 | 3% |
| Grade skipping | 0 | * |
| Early admissions | 0 | * |
| Credit by examination | 0 | * |

* not offered

new subject matter. In the category of lateral enrichment, Havighurst, Stivers, and DeHaan include art, music, drama, creative writing, and foreign language. Other writers include such examples as museum trips, mythology courses, and independent study programs as lateral enrichment. In relevant academic enrichment, or vertical enrichment, the students' age-grade levels are maintained and major subject matters are taught at an accelerated rate (Stanley 1976). In this type of enrichment, academic subjects such as mathematics, science, and reading are sequentially taught with materials appropriate to students' capacities, regardless of grade level. A number of advantages are claimed for in-class enrichment (Grossi 1980; Kough 1960; Renzulli 1977). It provides a means of specialized education for gifted/talented students in schools that are not large enough to hold specialized classes. Administratively, it is inexpensive and demands few changes in the classroom or school setting. Advocates of enrichment claim that this procedure allows gifted/talented students to stay with their own age-grade level and social and emotional peer groups where they can stimulate the non-gifted. It is also claimed that enrichment is more democratic than other administrative arrangements for gifted/talented students because it does not separate them into elitist groups. Teaching an enrichment program, based on individualized instruction, may lead to individualized instruction for all students in the classroom.

There are many disadvantages and reservations about in-class enrichments that have been cited by educators (Clark 1979; Fox 1979; Grossi 1980; Kough 1960; Renzulli 1977). Few teachers are well prepared to teach an enrichment program that demands knowledge of scope and sequence of a particular subject matter. Teachers do not have the background, available resources, or time to spend developing enrichment materials. In practice, most teachers tend to respond to slow learners demands for more time and gifted/talented students are, in effect, not challenged at appropriate levels of instruction. In-class enrichment is not always effective in that gifted/talented students are asked to put aside their needs except when enrichment activities are offered. The most common criticism of enrichment is that such programs are often simply improved education for all students and fail to address the advanced needs of gifted/talented students. Another common criticism is that, in the name of enrichment, programs offer inappropriate activities that are poorly related to the student's needs and interests (Grossi 1980; Renzulli 1977).

In the review of administrative arrangements used in contemporary programs, enrichment activities were cited in only 4 percent of the cases. Most developed art programs for the gifted/talented do not report using in-class enrichment. The curriculum in most programs for artistically talented students is idiosyncratic and viewed by the developers as enrichment to the students' general education. Havighurst, Stivers, and DeHaan (1955) listed art as an example of lateral enrichment, in which art activities are used to broaden students interests and range of activities in a non-accelerated program. Art is rarely viewed as a relevant academic enrichment subject matter that can be enriched and accelerated because few fully developed curricula exist. Accelerative enrichment is dependent upon an articulated curriculum such as the one suggested in Chapter 4, Part 2. It is a contemporary challenge for art educators to develop programs that can be enriched and accelerated for artistically talented students. Such programs must do more than offer "arts and crafts" activities without coherent relationships among the activities as we have suggested in Chapter I, Part 3.

## Ability Grouping

DeHaan and Kough (1956) offer the following definition of ability grouping: "*Ability grouping* refers to the device that brings the brightest

This charcoal sketch was done by an eighth-grade boy as part of an advanced art class in a junior high school. In this quick, three-minute, sketch the student captured the pensive mood and contours of the model. Though the chair is drawn incorrectly and the background is smudged, the drawing of the figure is very mature and belies the student's age. Photo by Indiana University AV Services.

pupils together for part or all of their academic work. This can take the form of special schools for gifted children, special classes within a regular school, special class periods where the gifted leave the regular classroom for part of their work, or ability groups within the regular classroom" (p. 12).

Ability grouping is often reported by many different terms such as multi-level grouping, multi-track programs, pull-out programs, honors programs, homogeneous grouping, cluster classes, and other terms. Whatever it is called, ability grouping, like enrichment, needs planned procedures and programs designed to serve the needs of gifted/talented students.

Advantages of ability grouping include the reduced range of individual differences, benefitting both students and teachers. Students in ability groups are more likely to explore and exchange ideas with greater group acceptance and can pursue advanced study in selected areas. Ability grouping also supports more opportunities for independent study, through special courses and non-school activities.

Disadvantages of ability grouping begin with its cost. Ability grouping requires special teachers, classrooms, and materials. It is also dependent upon having students with similar abilities in sufficient number to justify learning groups. Some critics claim that ability grouping encourages elitism or that it creates groups of students that are too concerned with achievement and competition. A concern expressed by some is that ability grouping removes stimulation from other students due to the removal of gifted/talented students into separate groups. Pull-out programs have become relatively popular but Clark (1979) expresses some concern about this form of ability grouping. Unless there is a cooperative relationship between teachers, students are often required to make up regular classroom work that took place during the pull-out. Some teachers resent the interruptions of students leaving and returning from pull-out activities. Another possible outcome is that pull-out participants may be isolated from other students due to the attention they receive elsewhere.

Art programs and students have suffered due to a major disadvantage of ability grouping as it is often practiced in schools. Academic areas such as science and mathematics are often dealt with through ability grouping and become identified as *the* gifted/talented program, therefore eliminating talent in the arts and other areas from consideration as gifted/talented programs. An effect of this practice is that students not gifted/talented in science and/or mathematics often do not consider themselves as gifted or talented. Art program leaders need to be aware that this situation exists in schools and that they need to create similar opportunities for artistically talented students such as special courses and other opportunities for superior students.

In the review of administrative arrangements used in contemporary programs, forms of ability grouping were cited in 75 percent of the 76 instances reported. This large percentage, however, includes a large number of out-of-school activities that take place in museums, summer schools, and Saturday classes. Out-of-school activities comprise 30 percent of all instances of administrative arrangements reported. It is by far the most popular administrative arrangements reported in current usage for educating artistically talented students. It appears that more educational opportunities are offered out of the schools than within school programs. Specialized schools are the next most popular administrative arrangement for artistically talented students. Arts magnet schools comprise most of the specialized schools reported. Many of these were created recently and art magnet schools appear to be growing in number across the country.

Acceleration

Acceleration was first used in St. Louis, Missouri, in 1868 and is the oldest administrative device used by schools. Acceleration allows students to "complete the standard academic work in less than the usual time" (DeHaan and Kough 1956, p. 11). Acceleration can include skipping entire grades, early entrance into various levels of schooling, doing more work than the normal amount expected during a school year, and doing advanced work for advanced standing.

Decades of educational writings have warned about social, emotional, and other adjustment problems in relationship to acceleration. Only recently, several persons have reviewed research and practices about the effects of enrichment and acceleration and these have shown consistently that the anticipated adjustment problems simply are not founded (Marland 1972; Daurio 1979; Fox 1979; Solano and George 1976). "Many educators and parents fear social maladjustment will ensue from moving ahead to be with an older peer group, and they also fear more important learning will be missed. Although the research indicates that these fears are not justified, this information has not been widely disseminated or understood" (Fox 1979, p. 114).

Daurio (1979) has pointed out that concern for social maladjustment among accelerated students is excessive and that there is "too little concern about the probability of maladjusting effects resulting from inadequate intellectual challenge" (p. 27). In recognition of these findings and observations, Fox (1979), Clark (1979), and others advocate that acceleration in some form should be available to all students in all gifted/talented programs.

One of the advantages of acceleration is that it requires a minimum of expenditures and can be used in any school. There are no special procedures required nor are special classrooms or material needed. Students who are in school for fewer years than other require less expense to parents, schools, and committees. Accelerated students are less bored in school and are more interested than other students in pursuit of their education. Acceleration allows students to progress at their own rate and enter their chosen field earlier than other students. Many writers have pointed out that gifted/talented students, by definition, are able to learn at faster rates than other students; acceleration is an appropriate accommodation to this characteristic. Some writers express reservations about acceleration because it fails to provide a special curriculum or program designed specifically for gifted/talented students. Past concerns about adjustment problems are still expressed as well as concern for missed content that will not be made up later.

Instances of acceleration comprise 21 percent of the total instances reported for the programs reviewed. Most of this acceleration occurred as non-graded groupings in out-of-school programs. Acceleration as a program is dependent upon a sequential, articulated curriculum so that students can progress through the curriculum at an accelerated rate. As we have pointed out previously, many programs for artistically talented students have not developed sequential curricula and, therefore, are unable to guide students through acceleration opportunities. An exception is offered in some high schools where Advanced Placement art courses are offered (7 percent in instances of the programs reviewed). It is as true in art as in other subjects that a student who can display competencies to be taught does not need more similar problems or projects; he or she needs to move ahead to more demanding and rewarding learning experiences.

## SUMMARY AND CONCLUSIONS

The terminology used to define and describe administrative arrangements for gifted/talented students is applied and reported inconsistently and is being changed or added to at all times. Nevertheless, most administrative arrangements can be categorized as types of enrichment, ability grouping, or acceleration. Programs for artistically gifted/talented students report infrequent use of enrichment, frequent and diverse means of ability grouping, and some limited use of acceleration. Forty programs for artistically gifted/talented students were reviewed, based upon program descriptions submitted to the authors, and their use of various administrative arrangements, by percentage of frequency, were reported. The four most frequently used administrative arrangements were out-of-school activities, specialized schools, accelerated progress, and pull-out classes. All others were reported by less than 10 percent of the programs reviewed. Each of the three major types of administrative arrangements (enrichment, ability grouping, and acceleration) were reviewed and advantages and disadvantages of each were discussed. It was pointed out that art teachers need to develop sequential curricula so that all three administrative arrangements can be offered for artistically talented students in more educational programs. Art teachers need to politically advocate recognition and inclusion of art programs as aspects of gifted/talented programs in the schools.

### Other Administrative Arrangements

Additional administrative and instructional provisions exist that were not reviewed in this chapter. These provisions can be used in almost any type of program for artistically talented students at any type of site. Some are especially suited to programs in smaller communities that lack specialized schools or other instructional resources. These include mentorships, internships, and traveling teachers based upon community resources.

### Mentorships

When a junior or senior high school is not able to provide advanced instruction, a mentor in the community can serve as a guide, role-model, teacher, and advisor (Grossi 1980). A mentor will have no organized agenda of instruction but will meet with students for a general sharing of ideas and guidance as part of a learning program (Fox 1979). Mentorship is similar to an apprentice-master relationship in which young people relate to a master craftsperson for an extended period of time. It includes shared responsibilities between the student and master and, therefore, careful matching of the student and master have to be arranged. The National Commission on Resources for Youth (1977) has published a guidebook for mentorship that includes criteria for selection and evaluation of mentors.

### Internships

Similarly, when a junior or senior high school is not able to provide advanced instruction for artistically talented students, internship opportunities should be explored. Internships can be arranged with individuals, agencies, and institutions for the purpose of implementing tasks that are required to accomplish specific outcomes in a student's area(s) of interest (Grossi 1980). Interns should spend extended periods of time, during or beyond the school day, with the sponsoring individual, agency, or institution with whom they are working. Internships offer career training opportunities not typically offered in the schools.

Two types of internships are job-shadowing and an apprenticeship. Job-shadowing is when learners "shadow" a professional in order to experience and observe the professional's work experiences and apprenticeship is when a student and a professional are paired. Local art programs can arrange such experiences for artistically talented students as part of their scheduled learning program. Administrative support of such internships is critical for their success with gifted/talented students.


### Traveling Teachers

Elementary schools that are relatively isolated or have small attendance and, therefore, are unable to form special classes or groupings for artistically talented students can arrange for the services of a traveling teacher in conjunction with other nearby schools or communities. Students can be given released time to pursue art activities with the traveling teacher individually or in small groups. Some schools who use traveling teacher services also provide a resource room specifically for this purpose.

These administrative options are being used in some programs for artistically talented students. Project Art Band at the DeCordova Museum arranges apprenticeships with artists in which young learners spend three hours per week, for ten weeks, working in artist's studios. The EXPAND program has both mentorships and internships that are based upon meeting individual student's needs. The Ferris Magnet High School, as part of Jersey City's Artistically Talented Classes, uses community resources as the basis of its mentor program. The EACH ART program uses a traveling art teacher to provide services to primary age children before they are eligible to enter the program's regularly scheduled classes.

A few states have recently legislated art requirements for high school graduation or art credit for college entrance. These states are critically examining art instruction as it is offered in schools and are asking for more, or clearer, delineation of sequences of skills and content learned in various art classes offered in the schools. California's *Visual and Performing Arts Framework* (1982) is an example of a state department of education's efforts to guide the development of coherent curricula and to expressly provide for the needs of artistically talented students who are in the California schools. According to the California Framework, artistically gifted/talented students must be encouraged to pursue their artistic potentials. For this purpose, the framework cites special scheduling of classes, accelerated placement, museum programs, artist-teachers, opportunities to teach younger students, and apprentice-type arrangements with designers and craftspeople as possibilities of administrative arrangements that might be made for artistically gifted/talented students. According to this framework, programs for artistically gifted/talented students should also provide in-depth studies in the roles and contributions of art critics, art historians, museum curators, archeologists, art collectors, architects, enviromental designers, and other professional roles in the arts beside that of the artist. These roles should all be studied, with a focus upon both the historical and the contemporary, to teach the broad contributions and significance of the visual arts in contemporary society.

These and similar claims and directives in recent documents from other states lead to recognition of the need for even more options in administrative arrangements for artistically talented students. Job-shadowing by advanced students, apprentice opportunities, career training and counseling, arts administration training and internships, and other options are only offered in a few generally isolated, specialist programs at schools, museums, or advanced summer institutes.

Gilbert Clark and Enid Zimmerman are shown with two teachers and a group of Indiana University Summer Arts Institute participants discussing and analyzing a contemporary sculpture. The study of art history, art criticism, and aesthetics are important aspects of any program for artistically talented students. Photo by Indiana University News Bureau.

6

*Looking Down the Road Ahead*

$\mathcal{R}$OBERT FROST'S WELL KNOWN POEM, The Road Not Taken (1915), about the differences that can be made in a person's life if he or she takes a less traveled road, is an apt metaphor for educating artistically talented students. How many gifted and talented young people have options to take the road less traveled by? It is easier to lead all students down the same path than to provide alternative roads that are less traveled. A basic premise of this text is that artistically talented students are a unique school population that deserve opportunities to take optional routes that will make a difference, not only to themselves but to society. Democracy means that each student should be able to reach his or her potential and should be provided the education and opportunity to make choices that lead to greatest possible development of individual gifts and talent. Such fulfillment of potential can only come about when the people of our nation, and their schools and government, make a commitment to educating the ablest in the arts as in other subjects.

## ISSUES OF PHILOSOPHY AND GOALS

$\mathcal{D}$ESIGNERS AND DIRECTORS of programs for artistically talented students need to confront and resolve many interrelated issues in the development of present and future programs. Design of programs for artistically talented students must begin with delineation of a consistent philosophy.

The philosophy of many programs is not based upon the individual needs of students in relation to their socio-political, economic, and cultural environments. They are based, rather, upon pragmatics of the moment, who is available to administer and teach and what resources are at hand. Decisions about program leadership and resources should be guided by a philosophy that is determined *before* the program is formulated or implemented. Comprehensive programs in the visual arts should include attention to society-centered, child-centered, and subject matter centered orientations in order to build social, personal, and conceptual-perceptual capabilities in students. Such programs should also attend to interrelationships among students, teachers, curriculum content, and settings in order to define differentiated educational programs and services that set them apart from those provided by the regular school program.


## ISSUES IN IDENTIFICATION


*I*DENTIFICATION OF ARTISTICALLY TALENTED STUDENTS for a program should be guided by the program's philosophy and goals. Program resources and funding will also effect the kinds of identification procedures used and the number of students selected to participate. A number of unresolved issues bear upon future identification procedures. Should art ability be measured in school-age youngsters? If so, how early can superior talent be identified? If identified early, does superior talent persist into adulthood or does it only emerge with maturity? If the latter, how early can superior talent be measured and identified? These questions remain unanswered. Much research is needed to resolve inconsistencies and contradictions about identifying artistically talented students.

Characteristics presently claimed to describe artistically talented students include many contradictory and inconsistent findings. Resolution of these problems requires attention to *both* the characteristics of art products and the behaviors of students as they relate to art making processes. At present, neither focus has been shown to be more effective than the other. Used in combination, they provide the best opportunities to identify artistically talented students both in terms of successful performance and its potential.

At present, there are a number of procedures that have been used to identify students for special programs in the visual arts. These procedures include standardized tests, informal instruments, and non-test measures. These and combinations of these procedures are generally not standardized and are used idiosyncratically throughout the country. In practice the use of non-test procedures far out-weighs the use of informal instruments or standardized tests. Most programs use some combination of procedures and self-nomination and portfolio review are the most popular. Based on present practices for identification of artistically talented students, it is clear that a battery of diverse identification instruments should be used. The use of many different procedures make it possible for a variety of expressions of talent to be recognized. Procedures presently used tend to be based upon locally defined criteria. As a result, procedures are not equivalent between programs and there is little common vocabulary upon which to base research and discuss issues relative to identifying talented students.

A new conception of talent in the visual arts is possible that parallels the concept of intelligence as a normally distributed construct. In such a concept, talent can be seen as occurring on a naive to sophisticated continuum in which every person can be viewed as having talent in varying degrees. This conception allows the construction of scales that could be created to measure naive to sophisticated expressions of talent.

Models for future development of identification procedures based upon visual art abilities as a distributed capacity and upon common criteria and vocabulary do exist, such as the Naive to Sophisticated Model (Clark and Zimmerman) and the National Assessment of Educational Progress: Art Assessment (NAEP). The Naive to Sophisticated Model can be used to define graded tasks and item content to measure many aspects and levels of art capacity and achievement. The NAEP Model offers standardized work-sample evaluation criteria and procedures for their application. Similar scales with greater differentiation between levels of achievement would facilitate identification of varying degrees of artistic talent, including superior abilities in the visual arts.

## ISSUES IN TEACHING

*I*T IS CLEAR THAT TEACHERS' PERSONALITY attributes, skills, points of view, and the instructional strategies they use are critically important for the successful teaching of artistically talented students. Selection of teachers for a program should not be guided by seniority or rank but by consistent application of the projected program philosophy. The program philosophy should also guide in-service activities that should be regularly scheduled parts of a program. Teachers can be taught to examine their personality attributes and skills and their instructional strategies to develop consistent application of the program philosophy and goals. Unfortunately, there is little research to guide teacher selection or retention. Most writing about teachers for gifted/talented students is purely speculative and fails to differentiate between good teachers and teachers best suited for gifted/talented students in general or for artistically talented students.

Differentiated educational programs for artistically talented students should include some use of different instructional strategies and teaching practices. There is some research indicating that ideal teachers for artistically talented students do need different skills than teachers for other groups, particularly competency in specific art making skills. Part of teacher in-service should include the examination and evaluation of teacher's beliefs, attitudes, values, and knowledge about artistically talented students. Teachers who know and understand the educational and other needs of artistically talented students are most likely to be successful in the instruction of such students. Teachers' roles and instructional strategies need to be planned as consistent with program philosophy, program goals, curriculum content, and administrative arrangements that support the program.

## ISSUES IN CURRICULUM CONTENT

*M*OST OF THE PAST as well as present recommendations about program content for artistically talented students have been directed toward art production activities. Content structures that are designed to meet the needs of all students, and artistically talented students in particular, should include art history, art criticism, and aesthetics, as well as art production as integral and balanced parts of the curriculum. Clark and Zimmerman's Naive to Sophisticated Model accommodates the need for a basic curriculum of learning experiences in the visual arts based upon artist, art historian, art critic, and aesthetician role models. It also provides structure for enrichment and acceleration opportunities as part of a program for artistically talented students. Expression of the model as a curriculum calls for the creation of curriculum units and learning materials that accommodate enrichment as in-depth learning within each role or between roles at any given stage and acceleration as breadth learning across stages.

There are a number of programs for artistically talented students across the United States and these programs share many similarities as well as structural and curricular differences. As the number of programs increases, it is apparent that an information sharing network among program personnel needs to be created. Such a network could provide needed information in support of program improvement and curriculum development at each site. There are more programs for artistically talented students at the senior high school level than at the elementary or junior high school levels. The art curriculum in all of these programs becomes more diverse, as well as specialized, as students increase in age and grade level. In the highest grades, a career training emphasis is often stressed. Traditional curriculum content is offered in most programs, such as drawing, painting, sculpture, ceramics, and printmaking with a heavy emphasis on art production activities. Such content provides an important basis for the study of and participation in less traditional art activities.

## ISSUES IN ADMINISTRATIVE ARRANGEMENTS AND SETTINGS

*D*ESPITE A FEAR OF ELITISM, research has consistently shown that artistically talented students profit most from being grouped with others like themselves. Programs for artistically talented students bring these students into contact with role models and career possibilities, as well as supportive a peer group. There are a growing number of programs offered in schools, museums, and other community settings despite minimal funding, support, and facilities. The most popular types of programs currently offered are in-school, magnet and specialized school, and summer school programs.

Within these and other types of programs, various forms of enrichment, ability grouping, and acceleration have been shown to be supportive and successful for artistically talented students. Which type of administrative arrangement is best and under what circumstances are issues that still remain to be resolved.

The most commonly used administrative arrangement in contemporary programs for artistically talented students is ability grouping. A limited number of acceleration opportunities and even less enrichment opportunities are provided. The following forms of administrative arrangements are used in the order listed: out-of-school activities, specialized schools, accelerated progress, pull-out classes, and others. Decisions about such program options need to be guided by consistency to the program's philosophy and goals rather than pragmatic considerations of administrative ease or convenience. A comprehensive program for artistically talented students requires formulation of a sequential, articulated curriculum as the foundation for planned administrative arrangements such as forms of enrichment, ability grouping, and acceleration. New conceptions of curriculum organization and administrative support systems are emerging in some visual arts programs; more need to be developed and implemented to create greater numbers of options and opportunities for artistically talented students.

# THE CHOSEN ROAD

*D*ESIGNING EDUCATIONAL PROGRAMS and services for artistically talented students requires simultaneous attention to many problems, some of which are unresolved. Some require commitment by the schools, some call for substantial change while others do not. Many will need to be researched and studied in many ways before new journeys can begin.

Efforts toward public support, program funding, development of teaching strategies, program content, and educational settings in the visual arts have lagged behind similar aspects of programs in other school subjects and activities. Most art teachers do not, at this time, have access to strategies and resources that would enable them to best educate their most talented students. As a result, in actual practice, great numbers of artistically talented students must seek instructional resources outside the school setting.

Review of the programs presently offered reveals a wide variety of means for student identification, teaching behaviors and strategies, curriculum content, and administrative arrangements and settings. At this time, it is difficult to find correct formulae to guide decisions about appropriate education for artistically talented students. The Marland Report (1972) established that, like all gifted/talented students, those who are artistically talented "require differentiated educational programs and/or services beyond those normally provided by the regular school program in order to realize their contribution to self and society" (vol. 1, p. 2). The development of such programs and services will demand attention to many interrelated aspects of educating artistically talented students.

We stand at a gateway in the education of artistically talented students. Ahead, there is a wide highway for most, some avenues that offer alternatives for special populations, and a few meandering footpaths for artistically talented students. The footpaths must be weeded, tended, straightened, and surfaced so that they will become attractive new roads for artistically talented students to travel.

# APPENDIX
## *Art Programs*

Listing is in Alphabetical Order by City

New York State Summer School of
the Arts
The State Education Department
Albany, NY 12234

Summer Enrichment Program
Department of Special Education
College of Education
The University of New Mexico
Albuquerque, NM 87131

The Archer M. Huntington Art
Gallery
The University of Texas at Austin
Austin, TX 78712

#415 Baltimore School for the Arts
712 Cathedral Street
Baltimore, MD 21201

Solo Art Shows
University of Cincinnati
Clermont College
Batavia, OH 45103

Indiana University Summer Arts
Institute
School of Education 002
Indiana University
Bloomington, IN 47405

The Magnet Art Program
English High School
77 Avenue Louis Pasteur
Boston, MA 02115

Boston University Visual Arts
Institute
225 Bay State Road
Boston, MA 02215

Texas Arts for Gifted/Talented
Department of Art, Box 207
West Texas State University
Canyon, TX 79016

School for Creative and Performing
Arts
310 Sycamore St.
Cincinnati, OH 45210

Enrichment and Acceleration for
    Children (EACH)
Whitehall City Schools
625 South Yearling Road
Columbus, OH 43212


Booker T. Washington High School
Arts Magnet High School
2510 Woodall Rogers Freeway
Dallas, TX 75201


Magnet Arts Program
Cass Technical High School
2121 Second Blvd.
Detroit, MI 48201


Weymouth Public Schools
200 Middle Street
East Weymouth, MA 02198


Frederick Junior/Senior High School
115 E. Church Street
Frederick, MD 21701


SUMMER ART
Department of Fine Arts
University of Northern Colorado
Greeley, CO 80639


Fine Arts Center
1613 West Washington Road
Greenville, NC 29601


Summer Unified Arts Program
North Grove Elementary
3280 W. Fairview Rd.
Greenwood, IN 46142


Tuesday Afternoons
9078 East D Avenue
Richland, MI 49083

Houston Independent School
    District
3830 Richmond Avenue
Houston, TX 77027


Art Enrichment Program
Washington Township and the
    Indianapolis
Museum of Art
Greenbriar School
8201 North Ditch Road
Indianapolis, IN 46260


Harcourt Elementary School
M.S.D. Washington Township
Indianapolis, IN 46240


Interlochen Center for the Arts
Interlochen Music Camp
Interlochen, MI 49643


Interlochen Center for the Arts
Interlochen Arts Academy
Interlochen, MI 49643


ESAA Magnet Program
Irvington Public Schools
1253 Clinton Avenue
Irvington, NJ 07111


Artistically Talented Classes
Jersey City Board of Education
241 Erie Street
Jersey City, NJ 07302


Ferris High School of the Arts
241 Erie Street
Jersey City, NJ 07302


Pennsylvania's Governors School
For the Arts
Box 213
Lewisburg, PA 17837

Project Art Band
DeCordova Museum
Sandy Pond Road
Lincoln, MA 01773

Shake Hands With Your Future
College of Education
Texas Tech University
Box 4560
Lubbock, TX 79409

Milwaukee Art Center
750 N. Lincoln Memorial Drive
Milwaukee, WI 53202

Milwaukee Magnet Program
Milwaukee Public Schools
P.O. Drawer 10K
Milwaukee, WI 53201

Walnut Hill School of the Perform-
    ing Arts
12 Highland Street
Natick, MA 01760

Jackie Robinson Middle School
New Haven Public Schools
New Haven, CT 06510

LaGuardia High School
PO Box 1812
Ansonia Station
New York, NY 10023

High School of Art and Design
1075 Second Ave. at 57th St.
New York, NY 10022

Bigelow Junior High School
42 Vernon Street
Newton, MA 02158

William Ward School
37 Iselin Terrace
New Rochelle, NY 10538

Norwalk School District
Norwalk, CT

Oklahoma Summer Arts Institute
Room 640
Jim Thorpe Bldg.
Oklahoma City, OK 73105

Florida School of the Arts
5001 St. Johns Avenue
St. Johns River Community College
Palatka, FL 32077

Cartwright School District
3401 N. 67th Ave.
Phoenix, AZ 85033

Dawes School
Pittsfield Public Schools
Pittsfield, MA 01201

Project Success: Art
North Kitsap School District 400
Poulsbo, WA

Advanced Placement Program
Box 2815
Princeton, NJ 08541

Arts Recognition and Talent Search
Educational Testing Service
Room D103
Princeton, NJ 08541

West Virginia Institute Arts and
    Crafts
Cedar Lakes
Ripley, WV

The Center for the Arts and
    Sciences
Ruben Daniels Life Long Learning
    Center
115 West Genese
Saginaw, MI 48602

Scholastic Awards
Scholastic Publications

Super Saturday
Department of Art Education/CA 1
Purdue University
West Lafayette, IN 47706

New Jersey School of the Arts
15 Forest Drive
Springfield, NJ 07081

Duke Ellington School of the Arts
35th and R Streets N.W.
Washington, D.C. 20007

New Trier High School East
385 Winnetka Avenue
Winnetka, IL 60093

North Carolina School for the Arts
200 Waughtown Street
Winston-Salem, N.C. 27107

Clark University School at
    Worcester
Arts Museum / Self Study Art
55 Salisbury Street
Worcester, MA 01608

# BIBLIOGRAPHY

Abraham, W. *Common sense about gifted children.* New York: Harper and Brothers, 1958.

Advanced Placement Program. College Board Editorial Office, 888 Seventh Avenue, New York.

Alexander R. An historical perspective on the gifted and talented in art. *Studies in Art Education,* 1958, 22 (2), 38–48.

Arnheim, R. *Visual thinking.* Berkeley, CA: University of California Press, 1969.

Arts Recognition and Talent Search. Educational Testing Service, Box 2876, Princeton, NJ.

Ashley, R. M. *Activities for motivating and teaching bright children.* West Nyack, NY: Parker Publishing Co., Inc., 1973.

Ayer, F. C. *The psychology of drawing.* Baltimore, MD: Warwick and York, 1916.

*The advocate survey: A survey of experts in education of gifted children.* Silver Spring, MD: Operations Research, 1971.

Barbe, W. B., and Frierson, E. C. Teaching the gifted: A new frame of reference. In W. B. Barbe (Ed.). *Psychology and education of the gifted: Selected readings.* New York: Appleton-Century-Crofts, 1965.

Barbe, W. B., and Renzulli, J. S. (Eds.). *Psychology and education of the gifted.* New York: Irvington Publishers Inc., 1975.

Barkan, M. Is there a discipline of art education? *Studies in Art Education,* 1963, 5 (2), 4–9.

Barkan, M., and Chapman, L. *Guidelines for art instruction through television for elementary schools.* Bloomington, IN: National Center for School and College Television, 1967.

Barkan, M., Chapman, L., and Kern, E. *Guidelines: Curriculum development for aesthetic education.* St. Louis: CEMREL, 1970.

Barnes, M. W. Enrichment in the elementary homerooms, Portland. In L. D. Crow and A. C. Crow (Eds.). *Educating the academically able.* New York: David McKay, 1963.

Becker, L. A. (Producer). *With eyes wide open, Richard Wawro, artist extra ordinem.* Austin, TX: Creative Learning Environments, 1983.

Bently, J. E. *Superior children.* New York: Norton, 1937.

Binet, A., and Henri, V. La psychologie individuelle. *L'Anée psychologique,* 1896, *2,* 411–465.

Binet, A., and Simon, Th. Méthodes nouvelles pour le diagnostic du niveau intellectuel des anormaux. *L'Annee psychologique,* 1905, *11,* 191–244.

Birch, J. W., and MacWilliams, E. M. *Challenging gifted children.* Bloomington, IL: Public School Publishing, 1955.

Bishop, W. E. Successful teachers of the gifted. *Exceptional Children,* 1968, *34* (5), 317–325.

Bloom, B. S. The master teachers. *Phi Delta KAPPAN,* 1982, *63* (10), 664–668, 715.

Boas, B. Creative art teaching: Is it in line with modern education theories? *Teachers College Record,* 1927, *28* (7), 723–28.

Boring, E. G. Intelligence as the tests test it. *New Republic,* 1923, *34,* 35–37.

Brandwein, P. F. *The gifted student as future scientist.* New York: Harcourt, Brace, World, 1955.

Brittain, W. L. Creative art. In L. A. Fliegler (Ed.). *Curriculum planning for the gifted.* Englewood Cliffs, NJ: Prentice-Hall, 1961.

Brittain, W. L., and Beittel, K. R. A study of some tests of creativity in relationship to performance in the visual arts. *Studies in Art Education,* 1961, *2* (3), 54–65.

Brown, R. *Social psychology.* New York: Free Press, 1965.

Bruner, J. S. *On knowing: Essays for the left hand.* Cambridge, MA: Harvard University Press, 1962.

Buros, O. K. (Ed.). *The nineteen thirty eight mental measurements yearbook.* New Brunswick, NJ: Rutgers University Press, 1938.

Buros, O. K. (Ed.) *The nineteen forty mental measurement yearbook.* Highland Park, NJ: Mental Measurements Yearbook, 1941.

Buros, O. K. (Ed.) *The third mental measurements yearbook.* New Brunswick, NJ: Rutgers University Press, 1949.

Buros, O.K. (Ed.) *The fourth mental measurements yearbook.* Highland Park, NJ: Gryphon Press, 1953.

Buros, O. K. (Ed.) *The fifth mental measurements yearbook.* Highland Park, NJ: Gryphon Press, 1959.

Buros, O. K. (Ed.) *The sixth mental measurements yearbook.* Highland Park, NJ: Gryphon Press, 1965.

Buros, O. (Ed.) *The seventh mental measurements yearbook.* Highland Park, NJ: Gryphon Press, 1972.

Buros, O. (Ed.) *Tests in print II.* Highland Park, NJ: Gryphon Press, 1974.

Buros, O. K. (Ed.) *The eighth mental measurements yearbook.* Highland Park, NJ: Gryphon Press, 1978.

Burt, C. The psychological aspects of aesthetic education. *Art Education,* 1967, *20* (3), 26–28.

Cane, F. The gifted child in art. *Journal of Educational Sociology,* 1936, *10* (2), 67–73.

Carroll, H. C. *Genius in the making.* New York: McGraw-Hill, 1940.

Center For Global Futures. *An identification and selection system for gifted and talented students.* Muncie, IN: Burris-Ball State School Corp., 1981.

Chaffee, E. General policies concerning education of intellectually gifted pupils. In L. D. Crow and A. Crow (Eds.). *Educating the academically able: A book of readings.* New York: David McKay, 1963.

Chapman, L. Curriculum planning in art education. *OAEA Journal,* 1970, *8* (1), 6–26.

Chapman, L. *Approaches to art in education.* New York: Harcourt, Brace, Jovanovich, 1978.

Clark, B. *Growing up gifted: Developing potential of children at home and at school.* Columbus, OH: Merrill, 1979.

Clark, G., and Zimmerman, E. A walk in the right direction: A model for visual arts education. *Studies in Art Education,* 1978a, *19* (2), 34–49.

Clark, G., and Zimmerman, E. *Art/design: Communicating visually.* Blauvelt, NY: Art Education, 1978b.

Clark, G., and Zimmerman, E. Toward a discipline of art education. *Phi Delta KAPPAN,* 1981, *63* (1), 53–55.

Clark, G., and Zimmerman, E. The gifted talented times. *School Arts.* A monthly column, 1982, 1983, 1984.

Clark, G., and Zimmerman, E. At the age of six I gave up a magnificent career as a painter: Seventy years of research about identifying students with superior abilities in the visual arts. *Gifted Child Quarterly,* 1983a, *27* (4), 180–184.

Clark, G., and Zimmerman, E. Comments: Programs for artistically talented students. *School Arts,* 1983b, *83* (3), 10–11.

Clark, G., and Zimmerman, E. Identifying artistically talented students. *School Arts,* 1983c, *83* (3), 26–31.

Clark, G., and Zimmerman, E. The Indiana University summer arts institute. In S. S. Madeja (Ed.). *Gifted and talented in art education.* Reston, VA: National Art Education Association, 1983d.

Clark, G., and Zimmerman, E. The Indiana University summer arts institute. *JEG,* 1983e, *5* (3), 204–208.

Clark, G., and Zimmerman, E. Towards establishing first class, unimpeachable art curricula prior to implementation. *Studies in Art Education,* 1983f, *24* (2), 77–85.

Cohen, H. L., and Coryell, N. G. (Eds.) *Educating superior students.* New York: American Book Co., 1935.

Cole, N. *The arts in the classroom.* New York: John Day, 1940.

Cole, N. *Children's arts from deep down inside.* New York: John Day, 1966.

Committee on Exceptional Children and Reporters of *Exchange* magazine, Metropolitan Study Council. *How to educate the gifted child: A collection of practical suggestions.* New York: Metropolitan School Study Council, 1956.

Conant, J. B. *The identification and education of the academically talented in the American secondary schools* (NEA conference report). Washington, DC: National Education Association, 1958.

Conant, H., and Randall, A. *Art in education.* Peoria, IL: Charles A. Bennett, 1959.

Cox, C. M. *Genetic studies of genius. Vol. 2, The early mental traits of three thousand geniuses.* Stanford, CA: Stanford University Press, 1926.

Cronbach, L. J. *Essentials of psychological testing* (2nd ed.). New York: Harper and Row, 1960.

Crow, L. D. Educating the academically able. In L. D. Crow and A. Crow (Eds.). *Educating the academically able,* New York: David McKay, 1963.

D'Amico, V. *Creative teaching in art.* Scranton, PA: International Textbook Co., 1942.

Daurio, S. P. Educational enrichment versus acceleration: A review of the literature. In W. C. George, S. J. Cohn, and J. C. Stanley (Eds.). *Educating the gifted: Acceleration and enrichment.* Baltimore, MD: Johns Hopkins University Press, 1979.

Davis, N. Teachers for the gifted. *Journal of Teacher Education,* 1954, *5,* 221–224.

DeCordova Museum *Project art band, a program for visually gifted children.* Lincoln, MA: DeCordova Museum, 1982.

Dehaan, R. Identifying gifted children. *School Review,* 1957, *65* (1), 41–48.

DeHaan, R. F., and Havighurst, R. J. *Educating gifted children.* Chicago: University of Chicago Press, 1957, 1961.

DeHaan, R. F., and Kough, J. *Teacher's guidance handbook: Elementary school edition volume 2 (Helping children with special needs).* Chicago, IL: Science Research Associates, 1956.

DeSaint-Exupéry, A. *The little prince.* New York: Harcourt, Brace, 1943.

Domonkos, A. Teaching art to young people: A new venture in the field of correspondence school instruction. *Art Education,* 1978, *21* (1), 15–17.

Doob, H. S. *Gifted students: Identification techniques and program organization.* Arlington, VA: Education Research Service, 1975.

Dorn, C. M. The advanced placement program in studio art. *Gifted Child Quarterly,* 1976, *20* (4), 450–458.

Drews, E. M. *The creative intellectual style in gifted adolescents.* East Lansing, MI: Cooperative Research Program No. E-2, 1964.

Efland, A. (Ed.) *Guidelines for planning art instruction in the elementary schools of Ohio.* Columbus, OH: State of Ohio Department of Education, 1970.

Eisner, E. Arts curricula for the gifted. *Teachers College Record,* 1966, *67* (7), 492–501.

Eisner, E. W. *Teaching art to the young: A curriculum development project in art education.* Stanford, CA.: Stanford University School of Education, 1969.

Eisner, E. W. *Educating artistic vision.* New York: Macmillan, 1972.

Ellison, R., Abe, C., Fox, D., Coray, K., and Taylor, C. Identifying artistic talent. *Gifted Child Quarterly,* 1976, *20* (4), 402–413.

Eng, H. *The psychology of children's drawings: From the first stroke to the coloured drawing.* New York: Harcourt Brace, 1931.

Erdt, M. H. *Teaching art in the elementary school.* New York: Holt, Rinehart and Winston, 1954, 1962.

Feldman, D. The mysterious case of extreme giftedness. In A. H. Passow (Ed.). *The gifted and the talented: Their education and development.* Chicago: University of Chicago Press (78th Yearbook of NSSE), 1979.

Feldman, E. B. *Becoming human through art: Aesthetic experience in the school.* Englewood Cliffs, NJ: Prentice-Hall, 1970.

Feldhusen, J. F. and Kolloff, M. B. A three-stage model for gifted education. *G/C/T,* 1978, *1,* 3–5, 53–58.

Fine, B. *Stretching their minds.* New York: E. P. Dutton, 1964.

Fine, M. J. Facilitating parent-child relationships for creativity. *Gifted Child Quarterly,* 1970, *21* (4), 487–500.

Fox, L. H. Programs for the gifted and talented: An overview. In A. H. Passow (Ed.). *The gifted and talented: Their education and development.* Chicago: University of Chicago Press (78th Yearbook of NSSE), 1979.

Freehill, M. F. (1961). *Gifted children: Their psychology and education.* New York: Macmillan, 1961.

French, J. L. *Educating the gifted: A book of readings.* New York: Henry Holt, 1959.

Fritz, H. E. A search for and conservation of the gifted. *Bulletin of High Points,* 1930, *12 (8)*, 19–25.

Friedenberg, E. Z. The gifted student and his enemies. In E. Z. Friedenberg (Ed.). *The dignity of youth and other atavisms.* Boston: Beacon Press, 1965.

Frost, R. The road not taken. *The Atlantic Monthly,* 1915, *116* (2), 223.

Gaitskell, C. D., and Hurwitz, A. *Children and their art* (2nd ed.). New York: Brace and World, 1970.

Gallagher, J. J. Social status of children related to intelligence propinquity and social perception. *Elementary School Journal,* 1958, *58* (4), 225–231.

Gallagher, J. J. *Teaching the gifted child* (2nd ed.). Boston: Allyn and Bacon, 1975.

Gallagher, J. J. Issues in education of the gifted. In A. H. Passow (Ed.). *The gifted and the talented: Their education and development.* Chicago: University of Chicago Press (78th Yearbook of NSSE), 1979.

Galton, F. *Hereditary genius.* London: Macmillan, 1869.

Getzels, J. W., and Jackson, P. W. The meaning of "giftedness"—an examination of an expanded concept. *Phi Delta KAPPAN,* 1958, *40* (2), 75–77.

Getzels, J. W., and Jackson, P. W. *Creativity and intelligence: Explorations with gifted students.* New York: John Wiley, 1962.

Goddard, H. H. *School training of gifted children.* Chicago: World Book Co., 1928.

Gold, M. J. *Education of the intellectually gifted.* Columbus, OH: Merrill, 1965.

Gold, M. J. Teachers and mentors. In A. H. Passow (Ed.). *The gifted and the talented: Their education and development.* Chicago: University of Chicago Press (78th Yearbook of NSSE), 1979.

Goodenough, F. *Draw-a-man test.* New York: World Book Co., 1926.

Goodlad, J. The curriculum. In J. Goodlad (Ed.). *The changing American school.* Chicago: University of Chicago Press (65th Yearbook of the NSSE), 1966.

Goodrich, H. B., and Knapp, R. H. *Origins of American scientists; A study made under the direction of a committee of the faculty of Wesleyan University.* Chicago: University of Chicago Press, 1952.

Gowan, J. C. Background and history of the gifted-child movement. In J. Stanley, W. C. George, and C. H. Solano (Eds.). *The gifted and the creative: A fifty-year perspective.* Baltimore, MD: Johns Hopkins University Press, 1977.

Gowan, J. C., and Demos, G. D. *The education and guidance of the ablest.* Springfield, IL: Thomas, 1964.

Grace, H. A., and Booth, N. R. Is the "gifted" child a social isolate? *Peabody Journal of Education,* 1958, *35* (4), 195–196.

Graves, M. *Graves design judgment test.* New York: Psychological Corp., 1946, 1974, 1978.

Greene, L. B. Creative art teaching and the gifted high school student. *California Journal of Secondary Education,* 1953, *28* (4), 197–202.

Grossi, J. A. Principles of differentiation of instruction. In J. B. Jordan and J. A. Gross (Eds.). *An administrator's handbook on designing programs for the gifted and talented.* Reston, VA: The Council for Exceptional Children and the Association for the Gifted, 1980.

Guilford, J. P. Creativity: Its measurement and development. In S. Parnes and H. Harding (Eds.). *A Source book for creative thinking.* New York: Scribner's, 1962.

Guilford, J. P. *The nature of human intelligence.* New York: McGraw-Hill, 1967.

Guilford, J. P. *Creativity tests for children.* Orange, CA: Sheridan Psychological Services, 1973.

Harris, D. B. *Children's drawings as measures of intellectual maturity.* New York: Harcourt, Brace, and World, 1963.

Havighurst, R. J. *The meaning of giftedness in education for the gifted.* Chicago: University of Chicago Press (57th Yearbook of NSSE), 1958.

Havighurst, R. J., Stivers, E., and DeHaan, R. F. A survey of education of gifted children. *Supplementary Educational Monographs,* 1955, *83,* 1–114.

Hawthorne, L. W., Speer, S. K., and Buccellato, L. Appropriateness of the Wechsler preschool and primary scale of intelligence for gifted children. *Journal of Consulting and Clinical Psychology,* 1983, *51* (3), 463–464.

Heck, A. O. *The education of exceptional children: Its challenge to teachers, parents, and laymen.* New York: McGraw-Hill, 1940.

Henry, T. S. *Classroom problems in the education of gifted children.* Bloomington, IL: Public School Publishing Company (19th Yearbook of NSSE), 1920.

Hildreth, G. H. *The child mind in evolution.* New York: Kings Crown Press, 1941.

Hildreth, G. H. *Educating gifted children at Hunter College Elementary School.* New York: Harper and Brothers, 1952.

Hildreth, G. H. *Introduction to the gifted.* New York: McGraw-Hill, 1966.

Hollingworth, L. S. *Special talents and defects.* New York: Macmillan, 1923.

Hollingworth, L. S. *Gifted children: Their nature and nurture.* New York: Macmillan, 1926.

Hopkins, L. B., and Shapiro, A. F. *Creative activities for the gifted child.* Palo Alto, CA: Fearon, 1969.

Horn, C. C. *The Horn art aptitude inventory.* Chicago: Stoelting, 1935, 1953.

Hoyle, E., and Wilks, J. *Gifted children and their education.* London: Department of Education and Science, 1975.

Hubbard, G. A. *Art in the high school.* Belmont, CA: Wadsworth, 1967.

Hurwitz, A. *The gifted and talented in art: A guide to program planning.* Worcester, MA: Davis Publications, 1983.

Inglehart, R. Identifying art talent. In B. Shertzer (Ed.). *Working with superior students.* Chicago: Science Research Associates, 1960.

Jackson, D. M. The emerging national and state concern. In A. H. Passow (Ed.). *The gifted and the talented: Their education and development.* Chicago: University of Chicago Press (78th Yearbook of NSSE), 1979.

Jacobs, J. C. Effectiveness of teacher and parent identification of gifted children as a function of school levels. *Psychology in the schools,* 1971, *8* (2), 140–142.

Jaensch, E. R. *Eidetic imagery.* London: Kegan Paul, 1930.

James, K. G. A report of the study in preparation of teachers for the gifted in elementary school. Doctoral dissertation, New York University, 1960.

Jardine, D. L. Correspondence school instruction as a foundation for careers in commercial art. *Art Education,* 1968, *21* (1), 17–18.

Jones, H. Phenomenal memorising as a special ability. *Journal of Applied Psychology,* 1926, *10,* 367–377.

Joyce, B., and Weil, M. *Models of teaching.* Englewood Cliffs, NJ: Prentice-Hall, 1972.

Kaplan, S. *Providing programs for the gifted and talented: A handbook.* Ventura, CA: Ventura County Superintendent of Schools, 1974.

Karnes, F. A., and Peddicord, H. Q. *Programs, leaders, consultants and other resources in gifted and talented education.* Springfield, IL: Thomas, 1980.

Kaufman, A. S., and Kaufman, N. L. *Kauffman assessment battery for children.* Circle Pines, MN: American Guidance Service, 1983.

Keating, D. P. Secondary school programs, issues concerning programs for the gifted and talented. In A.H. Passow (Ed.). *The gifted and the talented: Their education and development.* Chicago: University of Chicago Press (78th Yearbook of NSSE), 1979.

Kerschensteiner, G. *Die entwicklung der zeichnerischen begabung*. Munich: Gruber, 1905.

Khatena, J. *Music, art, leadership, and psychomotor abilities assessment records*. Starkville, MS: Allan Associates, 1981.

Khatena, J. *Educational psychology of the gifted*. New York: John Wiley, 1982.

Kik, C. Die übernormale zeichnenbegabung bei kindern. *Zeitschrift fur Angewandte Psychologie*, 1908, *2*, 92–149.

King, A. R., and Brownell, J. A. *The curriculum and the disciplines of knowledge: A theory of curriculum practice*. New York: John Wiley, 1966.

Klar, W. H., and Winslow, L. L. *Art education in principle and practice*. Springfield, MA: C. Valentine Kirby, 1933.

Kline, L. W., and Carey, G. L. *Measuring scale for freehand drawing: Part II, design and composition*. Baltimore, MD: Johns Hopkins University Press, 1933.

Knauber, A. *Knauber art ability test and Knauber art vocabulary test (published by the author)*, 1932, 1935.

Kolloff, M. B., and Feldhusen, J. PACE (program for academic and creative enrichment): An application of the Purdue three-stage model. *G/C/T/*, 1981, *18* (3), 4–50.

Kough, J. *Practical programs for the gifted*. Chicago: Science Research Associates, 1960.

Kough, Jr., and DeHaan, R. *Teacher's guidance handbook, elementary school edition Volume I: Identifying children with special needs*. Chicago: Science Research Associates, 1955.

Lark-Horovitz, B. On art appreciation of children: I. preference of picture subjects in general. *Journal of Educational Research*, 1937, *31* (8), 572–598.

Lark-Horovitz, B. On learning abilities in children recorded in a drawing experiment: I. subject matter and II. aesthetic and representational qualities. *Journal of Experimental Education*, 1941, *9* (4), 332–360.

Lark-Horovitz, B., Barnhardt, E. N., and Sills, E. M. Graphic *work-sample diagnosis: An analytical method of estimating children's drawing ability*. Cleveland: Cleveland Museum of Art, 1939.

Lark-Horovitz, B., and Norton, J. A. Children's art abilities: The interrelations and factorial structure of ten characteristics. *Child Development*, 1959, *30* (4), 433–452; 1960, *31* (1), 453–462.

Lark-Horovitz, B., Lewis, H., and Luca, M. *Understanding children's art for better teaching*. Columbus, OH: Merrill, 1967.

Laycock, S. R. *Gifted children*. Vancouver, British Columbia: Copp Clark, 1957.

Lazarus, E. *Project art band: A program for visually gifted children.* Lincoln, MA: DeCordova Museum, 1981.

Lee, J., and Lee, D. *The child and his curriculum.* New York: Appleton-Century-Crofts, 1950.

Lewerenz, A. S. *Test in fundamental abilities in the visual arts.* Los Angeles, CA: California Test Bureau, 1927.

Lindstrom, M. *Children's art.* Berkeley: University of California Press, 1957.

Lombroso, C. *The man of genius.* London: Walter Scott, 1895.

Lowenfeld, V. *Your child and his art: A guide for parents.* New York: Macmillan, 1954.

Lowenfeld, V., and Brittain, W. L. *Creative and mental growth.* New York: Macmillan, 1947, 1952, 1957, 1964, 1975.

Luca, M., and Allen, B. *Teaching gifted children art in grades one through three.* Sacramento, CA: California State Department of Education (ERIC Document Reproduction Service No. ED 082 433), 1974.

Lutz, F., and Lutz, S. B. Gifted pupils in the elementary school setting: An ethnographic study. Paper presented at AERA, Boston, 1980.

Madeja, S. S. (Ed.) *Gifted and talented in art education.* Reston, VA: National Art Education Association, 1983.

Maker, J. C. *Training teachers for the gifted and talented: A comparison of models.* Reston, VA: Council for Exceptional Children, 1976.

Manuel, H. T. *A study of talent in drawing.* Bloomington, IL: Public School Publishing Co., 1919a.

Manuel, H. T. Talent in drawing: An experimental study of the use of tests to discover special ability. *School and Home Education Monograph No. 3.* Bloomington, IL: Public School Publishing Co., 1919b.

Marland, S. P. *Education of the gifted and talented. Vol. 1. Report to the Congress of the United States by U. S. Commissioner of Education.* Washington, DC: USGPO, 1972.

Martinson, R. A. *Curriculum enrichment for the gifted in the primary grades.* Englewood Cliffs, NJ: Prentice-Hall, 1968.

Martinson, R. A., and Seagoe, M. *The abilities of young children.* Washington, DC: Council for Exceptional Children, 1967.

McAdory, M. *McAdory art test.* New York: Bureau of Publications, Teachers College Press, 1929.

McDonald, R. A. F. *Adjustment of school organization to various population groups.* New York: Teachers College Press, Columbia University, 1915.

McNary, S. R. The relationships between certain teacher characteristics and achievement and creativity of gifted students. Doctoral dissertation, Syracuse University, 1967.

McWilliams, E. M. Enrichment practices for gifted junior high school pupils. In J. L. French (Ed.). *Educating the gifted: A book of readings*. New York: Holt, Rinehart and Winston, 1964.

Mead, M. The gifted child in the American culture today. *Journal of Teacher Education*, 1954, *79*, 241–246.

Meier, N. C. *Aesthetic judgment as a measure of art talent*. Iowa City, IA: State University of Iowa, 1926.

Meier, N. C. *Meier art tests*. Iowa City, IA: State University of Iowa, Bureau of Educational Research and Service, 1929, 1942, 1963.

Meier, N. C. (Ed.). *Studies in the psychology of art. Vol III: Psychological monographs*. Iowa City, IA: University of Iowa Press, 1939.

Meier, N. C. *Art in human affairs*. New York: McGraw-Hill, 1942.

*Meier-Seashore Art Judgment Test*. Iowa City, IA: University of Iowa, 1930.

Meredith, P., and Landin, L. *100 activities for gifted children*. San Francisco, CA: Fearon, 1957.

Meumann, E. Ein program zur psychologischen untersuchung des zeichnens. *Zeitschrift fur Padagogische Psychologie*, 1912.

Meumann, E. *Vorlesungen zur einführung in die experimentelle pädagogik* (2nd ed.). Bd. 3. Leipsig: Englemann, 1914.

Miller, R. Social status and socio-empathetic differences among mentally superior, mentally typical and mentally retarded children. *Exceptional Children*, 1956, *23* (3), 114–119.

Mills, B. N., and Berry, G. L. Perceptions of decision-making groups towards the mentally gifted. *Educational Research Quarterly*, 1979, 4 (2), 66–67.

Morgan, J. J. B. *The psychology of abnormal people*. New York: Longmans, Green, 1936.

Morgan, H. J., Tennant, C. G., and Gold, M. J. *Elementary and secondary level programs for the gifted and talented*. New York: Teachers College Press, Columbia University, 1980.

Munro, T. *Art education: Its philosophy and psychology*. New York: The Liberal Arts Press, 1956.

Munro, T., Lark-Horovitz, B., and Barnhardt, E. N. Children's abilities: Studies at the Cleveland Museum of Art. *Journal of Experimental Education*, 1942, *11* (2), 97–184.

National Assessment of Educational Progress. *Design and drawing skills* (Art Report No. 06-A-01). Washington, DC: USGPO, 1977.

National Assessment of Educational Progress *Art and young Americans* (Art Report No. 10-A-01). Denver, CO: Education Commission of the States, 1981a.

National Assessment of Educational Progress. *Procedural handbook: 1978–1979 art assessment.* Denver, CO: Education Commission of the States, 1981b.

National Commission on Resources for Youth. *Community based mentorships for gifted and talented. Final report.* National Commission on Resources for Youth (Eric Document Reproduction Service No. Ed. 150 794), 1977.

Newland, T. E. *The gifted in socioeducational perspective.* Englewood Cliffs, NJ: Prentice-Hall, 1976.

Oden, M. The fulfillment of promise: Forty-year follow-up of the Terman gifted group. *Genetic Psychology Monographs,* 1968 77, 9–93.

Osburn, W. J., and Rohan, B. J. *Enriching the curriculum for gifted children.* New York: Macmillan, 1931.

Passow, A. H. Are we short changing the gifted? *School Executive,* 1955, 75 (4), 54–57.

Passow, A. H. (Ed.). *The gifted and the talented: Their education and development.* Chicago: University of Chicago Press (78th Yearbook of NSSE), 1979.

Passow, A. H., Goldberg, M. L., Tannenbaum, A., and French, W. *Planning for talented youth.* New York: Bureau of Publications, Teachers College Press, Columbia University, 1955.

Pegnato, C. W., and Birch, J. Locating gifted children in junior high schools: A comparison of methods. *Exceptional Children,* 1959, 25 (7), 300–304.

Peterson, J. *Early conceptions and tests of intelligence.* New York: World Book Co., 1925.

Peterson, N. *Project success in art (Introductory packet).* Poulsbo, WA: North Kitsap School District, Bureau of Elementary and Secondary Education, 1977.

Piaget, J. *Psychology of intelligence.* Totowa, NJ: Littlefield, Adams, 1966.

Pines, M. What produces great skills? Specific pattern is discerned. *New York Times,* C1–2, March 30, 1982.

P. L. 95-561. *The gifted and talented children's act.* Section 902, 1978.

Potok, C. *My name is Asher Lev.* New York: Alfred A. Knopf, Inc., 1972.

Pressey, S. L. *Educational acceleration: Appraisals and basic problems.* Columbus, OH: Bureau of Educational Research, Ohio State University, 1949.

Rader, J. Identification of the gifted and talented. Unpublished instrument, 1975.

Ragan, W. *Modern elementary curriculum.* New York: Dryden, 1953.

Renzulli, J. S. *The enrichment triad model: A guide for developing defensible programs for the gifted and talented.* Mansfield Center, CT: Creative Learning Press, 1977.

Renzulli, J. S., Smith, C. H., White, A. J., Callahan, C. M., and Hartman, R. K. *Scales for the rating behavioral characteristics of superior students: Artistic characteristics.* Mansfield Center, CT: Creative Learning Press, nd.

Rice, J. P. *The gifted: Developing total talent.* Springfield, IL: Thomas, 1970.

Robinson, H., Roedell, W., and Jackson, N. Early identification and intervention. In Passow, H. (Ed.). *The gifted and the talented: Their education and development.* Chicago: University of Chicago Press (78th Yearbook of NSSE), 1979.

Rubenzer, R. Identification and evaluation procedures for gifted and talented programs. *Gifted Child Quarterly,* 1979, *23* (3), 313–316.

Salome, R. A. Identifying and instructing the gifted in art. *Art Education,* 1974, *27* (3), 16–19.

Scheifele, M. *The gifted child in the regular classroom.* New York: Bureau of Publications, Teachers College, Columbia University, 1953.

Schubert, D. S.P. Intelligence as necessary but not sufficient for creativity. *Journal of Genetic Psychology,* 1973, *122,* 45–47.

Seashore, C. E. *Pioneering in psychology.* University of Iowa Studies, No. 398. Iowa City, IA: University of Iowa Press, 1942.

Selfe, L. *Nadia: A case of extraordinary drawing ability in an autistic child.* London: Academic Press, 1977.

Smith, B., Stanley, W., and Shores, J. *Fundamentals of curriculum development.* New York: World Book Co., 1957.

Solano, C. H., and George, W. C. College courses and educational facilitation of the gifted. *Gifted Child Quarterly,* 1976, *20,* 274–285.

Spaulding, R. L. What teacher attributes brings out the best in gifted children? Affective dimensions of creative processes. In J. J. Gallagher (Ed.). *Teaching gifted students: A book of readings.* Boston: Allyn & Bacon, 1965.

Stanley, J. C. Identifying and nurturing the intellectually gifted. *Phi Delta KAPPAN,* 1976, *58* (3), 234–237.

Stanley, J. C., George, W. C., and Solano, C. H. (Eds.). *The gifted and the creative: A fifty-year perspective.* Baltimore, MD: Johns Hopkins University Press, 1977.

Steiner, E. *Logical and conceptual analytic techniques for educational researchers.* Washington, DC: University Press of America, 1978.

Strang, R. *Guideposts for teachers of gifted children.* New York: Bureau of Publications, Teachers College, Columbia University, 1958.

Strang, R. Developing creative power of gifted children. In P. Witty, J. B. Conant, and R. Strang (Eds.). *Creativity.* New York: Bureau of Publications, Teachers College, Columbia University, 1959.

Sumption, M. R., and Luecking, E. M. *Education of the gifted.* New York: Ronald Press, 1960.

Tannenbaum, A. J. *Adolescent attitudes toward academic brilliance.* New York: Teachers College Press, 1962.

Tannenbaum, A. J. Pre-Sputnik to post-Watergate concern for the gifted. In A. H. Passow (Ed.). *The gifted and the talented: Their education and development.* Chicago: University of Chicago Press (78th Yearbook of NSSE), 1979.

Taylor, C. Using biographical information in identifying artistic talent. *Gifted Child Quarterly,* 1976, *20* (4), 402–413.

Teachers for the gifted. *Yearbook of special education: 1977–78 edition.* Chicago: Marquis Academic Media, Marquis Who's Who, 1977.

Tempest, N. R. *Teaching clever children 7–11.* London: Routledge and Kegan Paul, 1974.

Terman, L. M. Genius and stupidity: A study of some of the intellectual processes of seven "brighter" and seven "stupid" boys. *Pedagogical Seminary,* 1906, *13,* 307–373.

Terman, L. M. *Genetic studies of genius Vol. 1. Mental and physical traits of a thousand gifted children.* Stanford, CA: Stanford University Press, 1925.

Terman, L. M. The discovery and encouragement of exceptional talent. *American Psychologist,* 1954, *9* (6), 221–230.

Terman, L. M., and Burks, B. S. The gifted child. In C. Murchison (Ed.). *A Handbook of Child Psychology* (2nd ed.). Worcester, MA: Clark University Press, 1933.

Terman, L. M., Burks, B. S., and Jensen, D. W. *Genetic studies of genius. Vol. III, The promise of youth: Follow-up studies of a thousand gifted children.* Stanford, CA: Stanford University Press, 1930.

Terman, L. M., and Merrill, M. A. *Measuring intelligence.* Boston: Houghton Mifflin, 1937.

Terman, L. M., and Merrill, M. A. *Stanford-Binet Intelligence Scale: Manual for the third revision, Form L-M.* Boston: Houghton Mifflin, 1960.

Terman, L. M., and Oden, M. *Genetic studies of genius. Vol. 4. The gifted child grows up: Twenty-five years' follow-up of a superior group.* Stanford, CA: Stanford University Press, 1947.

Terman, L. M., and Oden, M. *Genetic studies of Genius, Vol. 5. The gifted group at mid-life: Thirty-five years' follow-up of the superior child.* Stanford, CA: Stanford University Press, 1959.

Thorn, D. A., and Newell, N. Hazards of the high I.Q. *Mental Hygiene,* 1945, *29* (1), 61–77.

Tiebout, C., and Meier, N. C. Artistic ability and general intelligence. *Psychological Monographs,* 1936, *48* (1), 95–125.

Todd, J. M. *Drawing in the elementary school.* Chicago: Laboratory Schools of the University of Chicago (#2), 1931.

Torrance, E. P. *Guiding creative talent.* Englewood Cliffs, NJ: Prentice-Hall, 1962.

Torrance, E. P. *Gifted children in the classroom.* New York: Macmillan, 1965.

Torrance, E. P. *Torrance tests of creative thinking: Norms-technical manual* (Research Edition). Princeton, NJ: Personnel Press, 1966.

Torrance, E. P. *Torrance tests of creative thinking: Norms-technical manual.* Lexington, MA: Personnel Press, 1974.

Tredgold, A. E. *A textbook of mental deficiency.* Baltimore, MD: William Wood, 1937.

Treffinger, D. J., and Gowan, J. C. An updated representative list of methods and educational programs for stimulating creativity. *The Journal of Creative Behavior,* 1971, *5* (2), 127–139.

Tuttle, F., and Becker, L. *Characteristics and identification of gifted and talented students.* Washington, DC: National Education Association, 1980.

Tyler, R. *Basic principles of curriculum and instruction.* Chicago: University of Chicago Press, 1950.

Varnum, W. H. *Selective art aptitude test.* Scranton, PA: International Textbook Co., 1939, 1946.

Vernon, P. E., Adamson, G., and Vernon, D. *The psychology and education of gifted children.* Boulder, CO: Viewpoint Press, 1972.

Viola, W. *Child art* (2nd ed.). London: University of London Press, 1942.

Visual performing arts curriculum framework and criteria committee. *Visual and performing arts framework for California public schools: Kindergarten through grade twelve.* Sacramento, CA: State Department of Education, 1982.

Waddell, J. H. Way of art for the gifted child, *Studies in Art Education,* 1960, *2* (1), 66–70.

Wallach, M., and Kogan, N. *Modes of thinking in young children.* New York: Holt, 1965.

Ward, V. S. *Educating the gifted: An axiomatic approach.* Columbus, OH: Merrill, 1961.

Ward, V. S. Program organization and implementation. In W. B. Barbe and J. S. Renzulli, (Eds.). *Psychology and education of the gifted* (2nd ed.). New York: Irvington Publishers, 1975.

Wechsler, D. *The measurement and appraisal of adult intelligence* (4th ed.). Baltimore, MD: Williams and Wilkins, 1958.

Wechsler, D. *Wechsler preschool and primary scale of intelligence (WPPSI).* New York: Psychological Corporation, 1967.

Weiner, J. J., and O'Shea, H. E. Attitudes of university faculty administrators, teachers, supervisors, and university students toward the gifted. *Exceptional Children,* 1963, *30* (4), 163–165.

Whipple, G. M. *Classes for gifted children.* Bloomington, IL: Public School Publishing Co., 1919.

Whittenberg, C. T. Gifted child in the normal classroom. *American Childhood,* 1954, *39* (9), 18–19.

Williams, F. *Classroom ideas for encouraging thinking and feeling.* Buffalo, NY: Dissemination of Knowledge Publishers, 1970.

Wilson, B. Little Julian's impure drawings: Why children make art. *Studies in Art Education,* 1976, *17* (2), 45–61.

Wilson, B., and Wilson, M. Visual narrative and the artistically gifted. *The Gifted Child Quarterly,* 1976, *20* (4), 432–447.

Wilson, B., and Wilson, M. Figure structure, figure action, and framing in drawings by American and Egyptian children. *Studies in Art Education,* 1979, *21* (1), 36–43.

Wilson, B., and Wilson, M. Instruments for the identification of artistically gifted. Paper presented at the National Art Education Association Convention, Chicago, 1981.

Wilson, M., and Wilson, B. *Teaching children to draw: A guide for teachers and parents.* Englewood Cliffs, NJ: Prentice-Hall, 1982.

Winner, E. *Invented worlds: The psychology of the arts.* Cambridge, MA: Harvard University Press, 1982.

Witty, P. A. *The gifted child.* Boston: D. C. Heath, 1951.

Witty, P. A., Conant, J. B., and Strang, R. *Creativity of gifted and talented children.* New York: Teachers College Press, Columbia University, 1959.

Worcester, D. A. *The education of children of above-average mentality.* Lincoln, NE: University of Nebraska Press, 1976.

Yochim, L. D. *Perceptual growth in creativity.* Scranton, PA: International Textbook Co., 1967.

Ziegfeld, Edwin (Ed.) *Art for the academically talented student in the secondary school.* Washington, DC: NEA/NAEA, 1961.

# AUTHOR INDEX

Abraham, W., 90, 91
Alexander, R., 151
Arnheim, R., 14
Ashley, R. M., 15, 43, 99, 101, 118, 119
Ayer, F. C., 7, 40, 56, 59

Barbe, W. B., and Frierson, E. C., 93
Barbe, W. B., and Renzulli, J. S., 82
Barkan, M., 28, 29
Barkan, M., and Chapman, L., 28
Barkan, M., Chapman, L., and Kern, E., 28
Barnes, M. W., 148
Becker, L. A., 46
Bently, J. E., 143
Binet, A. and Henri, V., 3, 4
Binet, A. and Simon, Th., 3
Birch, J. W., and MacWilliams, E. M., 58, 150
Bishop, W. E., 90, 91, 93, 94
Bloom, B. S., 11, 149
Boas, B., 15, 57, 60, 100
Boring, E. G., 38
Brandwein, P. F., 90, 91
Brittain, W. L., 15, 43, 100, 101, 118, 119, 122
Brown, R., 17
Bruner, J. S., 5
Buros, O. K., 8, 65, 66
Burt, C., 16

Cane, F., 41, 53, 56, 57, 119
Carroll, H. C., 91, 93
Chaffee, E., 145
Chapman, L., 28, 97, 99
Clark, B., 14, 27, 108, 146, 156, 158, 159
Clark, G., and Zimmerman, E., 19, 27, 29, 31, 34, 85, 99, 134, 145, 167, 168
Cohen, H. L., and Coryell, N. G., 145
Cole, N., 9
Conant, J. B., 91, 93
Conant, H., and Randall, A., 43, 53, 56, 58, 60, 91, 100
Cox, L. D., 5
Cronbach, L. J., 63
Crow, L. D., 90, 91

D'Amico, F., 9
Daurio, S. P., 159
Davis, N., 90, 93
Dehaan, R., 43
DeHaan, R. F., and Havighurst, R. J., 13, 59, 100, 101, 108, 119
DeHaan, R. F., and Kough, J., 100, 101, 118, 119, 156–58, 159
DeSaint-Exupery, 37
Domonkos, A., 101
Doob, H. S., 46, 53, 56, 58, 59
Dorn, C. M., 64
Drews, E. M., 90, 91, 93

Efland, A., 28, 99
Eisner, E., 8, 9, 15, 28, 65, 66, 67, 99, 122
Ellison, R., Abe, C., Fox, D., Coray, K., and Taylor, C., 80, 81
Eng, H., 7–8
Erdt, M. H., 100, 101, 119, 121

Feldman, D., 15
Feldman, E. B., 117
Feldhusen, J. F. and Kolloff, M. B., 113
Fine, B., 13, 109
Fine, M. J., 98
Fox, L. H., 100, 101, 156, 159, 161
Freehill, M. F., 121, 146
French, J. L., 90, 91, 93
Fritz, H. E., 14, 15, 41, 57, 58, 59, 100, 101
Friedenberg, E. Z., 91
Frost, R., 165

Gaitskell, C. D., and Hurwitz, A., 14, 43, 53, 56, 59, 99, 100, 101, 121
Gallagher, J. J., 13, 14, 27, 38, 78, 89, 90, 106, 148
Galton, F., 2
Getzels, J. W., and Jackson, P. W., 37
Goddard, H. H., 143, 151
Gold, M. J., 37, 38, 89, 90, 91, 105, 106, 119, 121
Goodlad, J., 42
Goodenough, F., 4
Goodrich, H. B., and Knapp, R. H., 90, 91, 93
Gowan, J. C., and Demos, G. D., 78, 89, 90, 91, 93, 102, 146
Grace, H. A. and Booth, N. R., 14
Graves, M., 8
Greene, L. B., 100, 101
Grossi, J. A., 155, 156, 161, 162
Guilford, J. P., 3, 4, 9, 16, 17, 40, 63, 64

Hall, G. S., 9
Harris, D. B., 4

Havighurst, R. J., 56
Havighurst, R. J., Stivers, E., and DeHaan, R. F., 43, 154, 155, 156
Hawthorne, L. W., Speer, S. K., and Buccellato, L., 4
Heck, A. O., 144
Henry, T. S., 91
Hildreth, G., 43, 57, 58, 90, 91, 93, 100, 101, 119, 121, 145, 147
Hollingworth, L. S., 14, 41, 44, 45, 58, 59, 60
Hopkins, L. B., and Shapiro, A. F., 118, 119
Horn, C. C., 8
Hoyle, E. and Wilks, J., 45, 46, 56, 58
Hubbard, G. A., 121
Hurwitz, A., 146

Inglehart, R., 43, 57, 58, 59, 67, 83, 84

Jackson, D. M., 15
Jacobs, J. C., 78
Jaensch, E. R., 46
James, K. G., 90, 91
Jardine, D. L., 101
Jones, H., 46
Joyce, B., and Weil, M., 99, 100

Kaplan, S., 108
Kaufman, A. S., and Kaufman, N. L., 4
Keating, D. P., 150
Kerschensteiner, G., 40
Khatena, J., 8, 27, 63, 64, 67, 73, 74, 78, 80, 84, 89, 146
Kik, C., 40
King, A. R., and Brownell, J. A., 29
Klar, W. H., and Winslow, L. L., 14, 41, 57, 59, 98, 100, 119, 121
Kline, L. W., and Corey, G. L., 8
Knauber, A., 8
Kolloff, M. B., and Feldhusen, J., 113
Kough, J., 146, 154, 155
Kough, Jr., and DeHaan, R., 43, 53, 56, 57, 58, 59, 60

Lark-Horovitz, B., 18, 42, 53, 56, 58, 59
Lark-Horovitz, B., Barnhardt, E. M.,
    and Sills, E. M., 18, 42
Lark-Horovitz, B., and Norton, J. A.,
    18, 22–23, 43, 53, 56
Lark-Horovitz, B., Lewis, H., and Luca,
    M., 18, 42, 53, 57, 58, 59, 60
Laycock, S. R., 15, 56, 98, 101, 121
Lazarus, E., 75
Lee, J., and Lee, D., 28
Lewerenz, A. S., 8
Lindstrom, M., 57, 58, 60
Lombroso, C., 2, 5
Lowenfeld, V., 9
Lowenfeld, V., and Brittain, W. L., 9,
    13, 44, 53, 56, 57, 58, 59, 60, 64, 98,
    101
Luca, M., and Allen, B., 14, 15, 47, 53,
    56, 57, 58, 59, 60, 99, 100, 101, 109,
    119, 121, 151
Lutz, F., and Lutz, S. B., 108


Madeja, S. M., 145
Maker, J. C., 90, 91, 93
Manuel, H. T., 7, 14, 41, 57, 58, 59, 60
Marland, S. P., 15, 27, 38
Martinson, R. A., 100, 101, 121
McAdory, M., 8
McDonald, R. A. F., 144
McNary, S. R., 94
McWilliams, E. M., 148
Mead, M., 108
Meier, N. C., 7, 8, 17, 41, 56, 57, 58, 65
Meredith, P., and Landin, L., 15, 118
Meumann, E., 17, 21, 22, 40
Miller, R., 14
Mills, B. N., and Berry, G. L., 108
Morgan, J. J. B., 46
Morgan, H. J., Tennant, C. G., and
    Gold, M. J., 146
Munro, T., 18, 42, 53, 56, 57, 58, 59, 60,
    100
Munro, T., Lark-Horovitz, B., and Barn-
    hardt, E. N., 42


Newland, T. E., 27, 31, 105

Oden, M., 5
Osburn, W. J., and Rohan, B. J., 119,
    121


Passow, A. H., 37, 90, 91, 93
Pegnato, C. W., and Birch, J., 45, 74, 78
Peterson, J., 17
Peterson, N., 46, 56, 57, 58, 59, 60, 121
Piaget, J., 17
Pines, M., 149
Potok, C., 111
Pressey, S. L., 150


Rader, J., 109
Ragan, W., 28
Renzulli, J. S., 27, 102, 112, 113, 122,
    148, 155, 156
Renzulli, J. S., Smith, C. H., White, A. J.,
    Callahan, C. M., and Hartman,
    R. K., 70, 80
Rice, J. P., 121, 146, 156
Robinson, H., Roedell, W., and Jackson,
    N., 15, 73, 74
Rubenzer, R., 63


Salome, R. A., 15, 38, 100, 101
Scheifele, M., 100, 101
Schubert, D. S. P., 14, 45, 58, 59, 108
Seashore, C. E., 7, 17, 41
Selfe, L., 45, 46
Smith, B., Stanley, W., and Shores, J., 28
Solano, C. H., and George, W. C., 159
Spaulding, R. L., 89
Stanley, J. C., 150, 155
Steiner, E., 29
Strang, R., 90, 91, 93
Sumption, M. R., and Luecking, E. M.,
    90, 91, 93


Tannenbaum, A., 42, 43, 45, 94, 108
Taylor, C., 80

Tempest, N. R., 15, 100, 101, 119
Terman, L. M., 3, 4, 5, 8, 14, 23, 40, 78, 145
Terman, L. M., and Burks, B. S., 5
Terman, L. M., Burks, B. S., and Jensen, D. W., 5
Terman, L. M., and Merrill, M. A., 3
Terman, L. M., and Oden, M., 5, 14
Thorn, D. A., and Newell, N., 144
Tiebout, C., and Meier, N. C., 7, 14, 42, 59
Todd, J. M., and Gale, A. V., 98, 100
Torrance, E. P., 9, 38, 64, 89, 108, 109
Tredgold, A. E., 45
Treffinger, D. J., and Gowan, J. C., 119
Tuttle, F., and Becker, L., 14, 73, 74, 80, 83, 84, 108
Tyler, R., 28

Varnum, W. H., 8
Vernon, P. E., Adamson, G., and Vernon, D., 14, 45, 46, 56, 58
Viola, W., 9, 15, 98

Waddell, J. H., 43, 46, 56, 58, 91, 100
Wallach, M., and Kogan, N., 9
Ward, V., 91
Wechsler, D., 3, 16, 17
Weiner, J. J., and O'Shea, H. E., 108
Whipple, G. M., 6, 7
Whittenberg, C. T., 100, 118, 119
Williams, F., 119
Wilson, B., 110–11
Wilson, B., and Wilson, M., 13, 47, 53, 56, 57, 58, 59, 80, 82, 84
Winner, E., 46
Witty, P. A., 14, 91
Witty, P. A., Conant, J. B., and Strang, R., 43, 46
Worcester, D. A., 151

Yochim, L. D., 43, 59

Ziegfeld, E., 14, 43, 57, 58, 59, 65, 66, 90, 91

# TOPIC INDEX

Ability grouping, 148–49, 156–59
Acceleration, 133, 140–41, 147, 150
Achievement tests, 10
Administrative arrangements: ability grouping, 148–49, 156–59; acceleration, 147, 150, 159–60; current issues, 169–70; history of, 143–51; in-class enrichment, 148, 149, 154; recommendations, 153–63
Advanced Placement Program in Studio Art and Art History, 64, 75, 160
Aesthetics, 29, 34, 119–22, 128, 134
Art and academic school records, 83
Art criticism, 30, 34, 60, 102, 119–22, 128, 131, 134
Art history, 29, 34, 119–22, 128, 131, 134
Art products: characteristics, 22–23, 48, 53–56; content of programs, 127–29, 131, 134; recommendations, 118–22
Art talent: 4, 13–25; definition, 38; distribution, 16–18; drawing, 6–9, 21–22, 40, 48; intelligence and, 13–18, 38, 41, 42; misconceptions, 14–15, 38
Arts Recognition and Talent Search, 75

Baker's Narrative Drawing Assessment, 64
Baker's Visual Memory Assessment, 64
Behavior checklists, 78–80
Biographical inventory: 80–81; case study, 110–11

California Achievement Tests, 10
California's Visual and Performing Arts Framework, 162–63
Case study, 100–11
Center for Global Futures, 63, 80
Characteristics of artistically talented students, 14, 46–48, 51–61
Child-centered orientation, 28, 30–31, 97, 98, 112, 117–18, 119
Child Study Movement, 9
Cleveland Studies, 18, 19–20, 42–43, 46
Creativity and self-expression tests, 9–10, 64–65
Current issues about educating artistically talented students, 165–71
Curriculum: art content model, 19, 27, 29, 133–41; current issues, 168–69; definition, 29, 34; orientations— child-centered, 28, 30–31, 117–18, 119; society-centered, 28, 30–31, 117–19; subject-matter-centered, 28, 30–31

Draw-a-Man Test, 4
Drawing: research about, 40–43, 48; skill, 21–22, 56; tests, 6–9

Enrichment, 133, 141, 147, 148, 149

*Genetic Studies of Genius,* 5, 8, 23, 145
Genius, 1–2
The Gifted/Talented Times (*School
  Arts*), 146
Gifted Talented Children's Act (PL 95–
  561), 38–39
Giftedness: 4, 38–39; categories of, 39,
  63–64, 70
*Goodenough Drawing Scale,* 41
*Graves Design Judgment Test:* 8, 64–65;
  critique of, 65
*Guilford's Creativity Tests for Children,*
  9, 64

*Horn Art Aptitude Scale,* 8, 63–64

Identification: by art products, 53–56; by
  student characteristics, 46–48, 56–60;
  current issues, 166–67; history of,
  37–49; recommendations, 73–85;
  research from 1900–1949, 40–42;
  research from 1950–1970, 42–44; research from 1971–present, 44–47
Idiot savant, 45
In-class enrichment, 148, 149, 154
In-school programs, 125–26
*Indiana University Summer Arts Insti-
  tute,* 31–34
Indicators of desire and interest, 83
Intelligence: art talent and, 13–18, 38,
  44–48, 58–59, 143–44; drawing ability
  and, 41, 42; measurement of, 2–4
Internships, 161–62
Interviews, 83
*IOWA Tests of Basic Skills,* 63

*Kaufman's Assessment Battery for Chil-
  dren (K-ABC),* 4
*Kline-Carey Drawing Scale,* 41
*Knauber Art Ability and Art Vocabulary
  Tests:* 8, 64–65; critique of, 65

*Lewerenz Tests in Fundamental Abilities
  in the Visual Arts,* 8, 41
Local art tests, 76

*McCarty Drawing Scale,* 41
Magnet and specialized schools, 125–26,
  153–54, 159
*Manuel Perceptual Learning Test,* 6
*Marland Report,* 15, 27, 38, 39, 63, 143
*McAdory Art Test,* 8, 41
*Measuring Scale for Freehand Drawing:
  Part II, Design and Composition,* 8
*Meier Art Tests:* 8, 63–64; critique of,
  66; *Meier Seashore Art Judgment
  Test,* 41
Mentorships, 161
*Metropolitan Achievement Tests,* 10
Misconceptions about art talent, 14–15,
  38
*My Name is Asher Lev,* 111

Nadia, 45–46
Naïve to sophisticated program model
  (N-S), 19–20, 22–23, 24, 29, 85, 135–
  40, 167
National Assessment of Educational
  Progress (NAEP): 18, 85, 167; Out-
  line of Art Objectives, 86–87
Nominations, 81

Observation as an aspect of identification, 84
Out-of-school programs, 125–26, 154, 159

Philosophy and goals: 27, 31, 73, 102,
  105–11, 112–14, 129–31, 133–35; current issues, 165–71; program emphases, 126–27
Program content, 127–29, 133–41
Program structures: in-school-programs,
  125–26; magnet and specialized

Program structures (*cont.*)
    schools, 125–26, 153–54, 159; out-of-
    school programs, 125–26, 154, 159;
    school/museum programs, 126, 153–
    54; summer programs, 125–26, 154,
    159
Progressive Education Movement, 145
Portfolio review, 75
Program model for artistically talented
    students: 29–32; naïve to sophisti-
    cated program model (N-S), 19–20,
    22–23, 24, 29, 85, 135–40, 167
Purdue Three-Stage Model (Feldhusen &
    Kolloff), 113

Renzulli Enrichment Triad Model, 112
*Renzulli Scales for the Rating Behavioral
    Characteristics of Superior Students:
    Artistic Characteristics,* 68, 70

School/museum programs, 126, 153–54
*Seashore Measures of Musical Talent,* 63
*Selective Art Aptitude Test,* 8
Selection criteria for teachers, 105–06
Self-interest inventory, 80–81
*The Seven Drawing Test,* 42
*Stanford Achievement Tests,* 10
*Stanford-Binet Intelligence Scale,* 5, 8, 38,
    63, 74
*Steacy Drawing Construction Tests,* 6
Structure of the Intellect Model, (SOI),
    64
Structured nominations, 78
Society-centered orientation, 28, 30–31,
    97, 98, 112, 117–19
Student characteristics, 46–48, 56–60
Student/teacher interactions, 101
*SRA Achievement Series,* 10
Subject-matter-centered orientation, 28,
    30–31, 97, 99, 112
Summer programs, 125–26, 154, 159

Teacher characteristics: current issues,
    167–68; history of inquiry, 89–94;
    recommendations, 105–15; selection
    criteria, 105–06; values and attitudes,
    167–68
Teaching strategies: 91–93, 97; current
    issues, 167–68; curriculum planning,
    100; media and instructional materi-
    als, 101; orientations — child-centered,
    97, 98, 112; society-centered, 97, 98,
    112; subject-matter-centered, 97, 99,
    112; practices, 111–15; teacher/student
    interactions, 101
Testing art abilities: history of, 6–9; in-
    formal instruments, 63, 67–70, 74–
    81, 84; non-test measures, 63, 67–70,
    81–84, 84; standardized tests, 63, 65–
    67, 74, 84
*Thorndike's Esthetic Appreciation Test,*
    6
*Torrance Self-Awareness Checklist,* 109
*Torrance Test of Creative Thinking,* 9,
    38, 64
Traveling teachers, 162

United States Office of Education: cate-
    gories of giftedness, 39, 63–64, 70

Values and attitudes of teachers, 167–68

*Wechsler Adult Intelligence Scale (WAIS),*
    3
*Wechsler Intelligence Scale for Children
    (WISC),* 3, 38
*Wechsler Preschool and Primary Scale of
    Intelligence (WPPSI),* 3
Work-sample technique, 43, 44, 47, 48

EDUCATING ARTISTICALLY TALENTED STUDENTS

was composed in 10-point Digital Compugraphic Sabon and leaded two points,
with display type in Sabon with Caslon Special initials,
by Metricomp and Dix Typesetting Co., Inc.;
printed by sheet-fed offset on 50-pound, acid-free Warren Eggshell Cream,
Smythe-sewn, and bound over binder's boards in Joanna Arrestox B,
by Maple-Vail Book Manufacturing Group, Inc.;
and published by

SYRACUSE UNIVERSITY PRESS
SYRACUSE, NEW YORK 13210